JOSEPH CONRAD

MEN AND BOOKS

JOSEPH
CONRAD

by

OLIVER WARNER

LONGMANS, GREEN AND CO
LONDON · NEW YORK · TORONTO

LONGMANS, GREEN AND CO LTD
6 & 7 CLIFFORD STREET LONDON W I

ALSO AT MELBOURNE AND CAPE TOWN

LONGMANS, GREEN AND CO INC
55 FIFTH AVENUE NEW YORK 3

LONGMANS, GREEN AND CO
215 VICTORIA STREET TORONTO I

ORIENT LONGMANS LTD
BOMBAY CALCUTTA MADRAS

First published in 1951

PRINTED IN GREAT BRITAIN
BY WESTERN PRINTING SERVICES, LTD., BRISTOL

To

GEOFFREY AND BARBARA OLIVER
this study of a man who found
enchantment in Eastern seas

'Everything you say I shall remember in my heart.'—Thaddeus Bobrowski to Joseph Conrad

PREFACE

THERE are many still living who knew Joseph Conrad. Among them, some have recorded impressions of his personality and achievement in books which are invaluable, for no writer had stauncher friends or more discriminating admirers. Above all, in M. Jean-Aubry he had a delightful biographer; a French writer with an affectionate understanding and a clear style. To the two volumes of his *Life and Letters* any further general work on Conrad is certain to be indebted: there could be no honourable exception.

In acknowledging the obligation necessarily incurred to many forerunners, the point perhaps needs making that the difference in mental climate between 1924, the year in which Conrad died, and the present is far greater than the actual span of time could suggest. It is the true justification for a new survey of the whole of his published work. No two critics will ever quite agree about a writer of consequence—except perhaps in one respect, the pleasure that he gives; and even that will differ, in kind and in degree. But it is important common ground. Walter Sickert indeed said that, in his view, 'pleasure, and pleasure alone, is the proper purpose of art'. The reader of Conrad who does not largely concur will probably have laid his work down at an early stage. It is not the whole story, but it is a vital part of it, and it is possibly best amplified by a quotation from the Author's Note to later editions of *The Nigger of the 'Narcissus'*.

'The changing wisdom of successive generations', says

Conrad, 'discards ideas, questions facts, demolishes theories. But the artist appeals to that part of our being which is not dependent on wisdom: to that in us which is a gift and not an acquisition—and, therefore, more permanently enduring. He speaks to our capacity for delight and wonder, to the sense of mystery surrounding our lives; to our sense of pity, and beauty, and pain; to the latent feeling of fellowship with all creation—and to the subtle but invincible conviction of solidarity that knits together the loneliness of innumerable hearts; to the solidarity in dreams, in joy, in sorrow, in aspirations, in illusions, in hope, in fear, which binds men to each other, which binds together all humanity—the dead to the living and the living to the unborn.'

It is as well for any writer to make clear his attitude to his subject. The pages which follow are an attempt at appreciation. Conrad had limitations and imperfections, as all men have. He was at times intolerant, and he sometimes strained the tension of a story further than the theme warranted. But he was an artist of such quality that even those such as Henry James, who (if what Ford Madox Ford says is true) were at heart somewhat antipathetic to him, yet felt 'an immense respect both for his character and achievements'.

The admiration is shared, without serious qualification, by the present writer.

ACKNOWLEDGMENTS

Quotations in the text from Conrad's books and letters are made by permission of Messrs. J. M. Dent and Sons Ltd., as Agents for the Trustees of the Author's Estate.

Invaluable advice, bibliographically, has been given by Mr. John Hayward, by the Secretary of the Conrad Polish Club in London, and through the good offices of the British Council.

CONTENTS

xi

ILLUSTRATIONS

POLAND

I

THE Poland where Conrad was born was a land of memories and sorrows. John Sobieski, her last great king, had in 1683 saved Vienna from the Turk, but his realm, large and unstable, faced in the eighteenth century two formidable powers, the Russian Empire as Peter the Great had left it, and a rising Prussia. Austria, though involved in the south-east, and taxed by her effort to maintain supremacy in Central Germany, offered further challenge.

The Polish monarchy was elective; succession a cause of intrigue, corruption, often of rebellion on the part of her nobles; and it was fated that, while the country should be led by no further John Sobieskis, the reign of the ablest Hohenzollern, Frederick the Great, should coincide with the ablest successor of Peter—the Empress Catherine. As a strong and independent Poland thwarted alike the consolidation of Prussia and the advance of Russia into the heart of Europe, her doom, under weak or divided leadership, was certain. She was eliminated in three stages.

The partitions of 1772, 1793, and 1795 in which Russia, Prussia, and Austria took part, dissolved a kingdom which had been renowned in Europe since the

thirteenth century. With an irony which all thinking
Poles felt to the full, the division re-created that spirit
of nationality which, in the days of her independence,
had been called into play too often merely to serve
dynastic or local ends. Now that she had been sundered
from without, self-awareness grew and deepened.
During the century which followed, the Poles, however
oppressed, never lost the hope that their fortunes would
one day be restored. Their aspiration was fulfilled at
last as a consequence of the first world war, which
Conrad himself lived to see. After two decades it was
followed by a fourth partition and, later, by a new
restoration.

In the early years of the nineteenth century Napoleon
had established a Grand Duchy of Warsaw, in an attempt
to weaken Austria and Prussia; and at the Congress of
Vienna, when his Europe was revised, the Tsar Alexander I
wished to create an autonomous Polish state under
Russian suzerainty. This was indeed set up, but it
covered a diminished country. Prussia retained Thorn,
Danzig and the modern province of Pozen; Austria
recovered Eastern Galicia. Cracow, with a strip of
territory, was established as an independent republic.
In effect, the dismemberment was maintained. Auto-
nomy in Russian Poland was continued only until the
revolution of 1830–1, on the failure of which the con-
stitution granted in 1815 after Vienna was withdrawn.
The free republic of Cracow lasted fifteen years longer,
when it was annexed by Austria. Conrad's birth, therefore, coincided with a time of deep depression in his
country; and every circumstance of his early years con-
spired to make him aware of the political tragedy to
which he and his compatriots were heirs.

He was born at Berdyczew on 3 December 1857,

his full names being Josef Teodor Konrad Nalecz Korzeniowski. The bare facts of his immediate heredity were recorded by himself in a letter to Edward Garnett dated 20 January 1900, one purpose of which was to show his literary genealogy, such as it was. The letter, incidentally, is notable for a number of small slips in tense which were a feature of almost all Conrad's writing. They were symptomatic of his memory, in which detail was often obliterated. His wife remarked that he always insisted on a wildly inaccurate date when recalling their marriage. Time, with him, took a strictly relative place.

Conrad explains at the beginning of the letter that his surname derived from the Polish word for *root*, which to him was not without its significance. 'Land-tilling gentry' was how he described both the Korzeniowskis and his mother's family, the Bobrowskis.

'My paternal grandfather,' said Conrad, 'Teodor N. Korzeniowski, served in the cavalry. Decorated with the cross of "Virtuti Militari" . . . something in the nature of V.C. Attained the rank of Captain in 1830 when the Russo-Polish war occurred, after which the so-called Polish Army ceased to exist. Two wounds. Retired to a little hereditary estate. . . . Wrote a tragedy in five acts, verse, privately printed and so extremely dull that no one was ever known to have read it through. I know I couldn't, notwithstanding my family pride and the general piety of my disposition.

'My other grandfather,' he continued, 'Joseph Bobrowski, man of wit, owner of a famous stud of Steppe horses, lived and died on his estate of Oratow: popular, greatly lamented. Never wrote but letters (and very few of these) and a large number of promissory notes dedicated to various Jews. Left a large family of sons and one daughter, Eva (Evelina)—my mother. There was an extraordinary sister-cult in that family, from which I profited when left an orphan . . . and my mother certainly was no ordinary woman. Her correspondence with my father and with her brothers which in the year 1890 I have read and afterwards destroyed, was a revelation to me; I shall never forget my delight, admiration and unutterable regret at my loss (before I could appreciate her), which only then I fully understood. One of her brothers, Thaddeus, to whom I stand more in the relation of a son than of a nephew, was a man of powerful intelligence and great force of character and possessed of an enormous influence in the Three Provinces (Ukraine, Volhynia and Podolia). A most distinguished man. Another, Stephen, was in 1862 Chief of the Polish Revolutionary Committee in Warsaw.' This uncle was killed in a duel with a political opponent. Another, on his father's side, Robert Korzeniowski, was killed in an abortive rising of 1863. Yet another, Hilary Korzeniowski, was exiled to Siberia for his part in it, and died there ten years later.

Conrad continued, as if to emphasize the strangeness of his own particular gifts, that none of the members of the many families to which his two grandfathers were related was literary, but that 'all made sacrifices of fortune, liberty and life for the cause in which they believed; and very few had any illusions as to its success.'

In the same letter there is a sketch of his father: Apollonius, or more usually, Apollo Korzeniowski: 'Educated in the University of St. Petersburg, Department of Oriental Studies and Philology. No degree. Debts. Social successes and any amount of *bonnes fortunes*. Poet . . . Arrested in 1862 and . . . condemned to deportation into Russia. . . . My mother

died in exile. My father liberated in '67 on the repre-
sentation of Prince Gallitzin that he was no longer
dangerous.'

Conrad mentions his father's translations; they included Hugo's *Travailleurs de la Mer* and five plays of
Shakespeare: *Much Ado About Nothing*, *As You Like It*,
The Two Gentlemen of Verona, *A Comedy of Errors* and
Othello. 'Some of these,' he says, 'I read when I could
not have been more than eight or nine years old.' His
first acquaintance with Dickens, another admiration of
his father, began almost as early.

The sketch of Apollo concludes: 'A man of great
sensibilities; of exalted and dreamy temperament; with
a terrible gift of irony and of gloomy disposition; withal,
of strong religious feeling, degenerating after the loss of
his wife into mysticism touched with despair. His
aspect was distinguished; his conversation very fascinating; but his face, in repose sombre, lighted all over when
he smiled. I remember him well. For the last two years
of his life I lived alone with him. . . .'

Thaddeus Bobrowski adds the following note about the
Korzeniowski family, for whom his admiration was
qualified, his own people having originally been against
the match between Conrad's father and mother: 'Your
grandfather and uncle,' he wrote to his young nephew,
'were always entertaining projects which had no validity
except in their imaginations. . . . Your father was an
idealistic dreamer; he loved mankind and wished them
well; but he had two standards for judging them. He
was indulgent to the poor, and very hard on the rich.'

It is not inappropriate to describe Conrad's early days
in bold outline, for the salient facts are clear and tragic
in the personal as in the wider sense. Conrad himself
was usually reticent about them. He drew in some detail

on childhood memories in *A Personal Record*,[1] but detail
is the word, for the wider background was intractable,
and of almost unrelieved gloom. In fact, both his parents
died largely as a result of hardships in exile, his mother
in 1865 when he was seven, and his father four years
later.

Early years and heredity were of enormous importance,
as they always must be, in the making of Conrad's
character, in the quality of his gifts, and in his outlook
upon the world. To begin with, novelists should be
generous dreamers, unless they are content to be mere
reporters of the life around them. Conrad knew none
but such people; men and women whose most vivid life
was that of the imagination; thwarted folk who tried to
make up in abundance of aspiration for what was denied
them in cruel reality. Added to this were literary pre-
dilections certainly inherited from his father but furthered by the loneliness of much of his boyhood. As a
child, although he never lacked warmth of companionship, he was often completely cut off from his contemporaries, and had to rely upon older people for such
entertainment as came his way. It was generally of a
sober kind.

Three outstanding characteristics he certainly owed to
his upbringing. The first was his intense loyalty to those
who were dear to him. This was unshakable. Again it
was both personal and national. The Poles felt themselves surrounded by enemies, as indeed they were. It
gave them a feeling of kinship which they lost all too
easily in days of greater prosperity. For this reason, they
cherished, more than ever before, their language. It is
not an easy one, but Conrad himself, though for much the

---

[1] Published originally, in book form, as *Some Reminiscences* (1912); Conrad
afterwards changed the title to *A Personal Record*.

greater part of his life he had no occasion to use it, had it always at command, wrote it well and, in times of delirium, in his bouts of illness, spoke it. It was almost a secret cult, for the Russians did their utmost to suppress it, and a cousin of Conrad's, Stanislaus Bobrowski, received a sentence of eighteen months in jail for giving lessons in his mother tongue.

Conrad's mastery of language depended upon memory, and in this respect his endowment was peculiar. His carelessness in detail has been noted; moreover he wrote in *A Personal Record*: 'I never made a note of a fact, of an impression or of an anecdote in my life.' In spite of this natural weakness and the absence of any form of record to counter it, he could yet, when need arose, re-create a substantial fragment of autobiography perfect in verisimilitude. His was, in fact, a visual memory, to which was added the gift of what might be called mental tenacity. This enabled him to keep his Polish faultless, though often long unused, as well as the French of his adolescence and even to some extent the German he learnt at school. Of his French, M. Jean-Aubry said: 'Conrad's knowledge was perfect. He not only spoke correctly . . . but he showed . . . as a literary man, a nice feeling for French style and a knowledge of precise meanings of words which many Frenchmen might have envied.' There is a whole published volume of his letters written in that language. As for his acquisition and later command of English, at a stage of life when learning had necessarily become less easy, it is one of the smaller miracles of literature.

Conrad's uncommon education, and the fact that from a very early age he was an omnivorous reader, gave him exceptional range in purely literary knowledge. Shakespeare and Dickens he knew through the translations and the library collected by his father, and he became more widely read in the literature of the country he came to adopt than most Englishmen. Polish letters he had thoroughly explored, including the work of another Joseph Korzeniowski, not a relation, who died in 1863 after having written novels of country life, together with poems and plays. With the greater French writers Conrad was on familiar terms. He read little in German and knew no Russian, 'not even the alphabet,' as he used to say with emphasis, but he had read, in translation, the greater novelists of that country. Of Dostoievski he spoke with distaste, for not only did Dostoievski dislike the Poles, but, as Mr. Richard Curle once shrewdly remarked, 'perhaps he saw in this Russian the most formidable of all antagonists to his own theories of a world governed by sanity and method.'

Lastly, although he complained in print that he was badly taught in geography, experience brought him thorough acquaintance with a large part of the physical world. Added to all this, he was reasonably knowledgeable in Latin, and was never at a loss for an allusion in classical mythology.

In fact, if he was born and nurtured in an atmosphere of sorrow, bitterness and some actual hardship, the compensations were considerable—for an artist. In certain respects, and they were important ones, no writer has ever been better equipped.

The story of his childhood peregrinations is as follows. Immediately after their marriage, Conrad's parents lived for a while on an estate in the neighbourhood of Luczyniec, in Podolia, which Apollo managed. After his wife's dowry of eight thousand roubles had been paid, Apollo rented a property in the jurisdiction of Mohilow, where their only child was born, and where they lived until the end of the year 1859. The venture was not a success, and the family moved to Jitomir, a short distance away, where Apollo hoped he might turn to profit his gifts as a translator and literary critic. There they lived for some two years, and there Conrad was baptized into the Church of Rome.

Early in 1862 Apollo was induced to settle in Warsaw by the many friends he had there. He had hopes—never realized—of starting a fortnightly review. His wife and child joined him in the autumn of the same year. Evelina probably knew that one of the main reasons for Apollo's move was that he should help in organizing a secret national committee, whose ultimate aim was to win back independence from Russia. A premature insurrection actually took place in Warsaw in January 1863, and although Apollo did not himself take active part in it, the Russians knew by their spies of the clandestine meetings which had taken place in his house, and of his wife's continual wearing of the forbidden black—a token of national mourning.

Apollo was, in fact, arrested and imprisoned in the citadel. Later, by sentence of a military court, he was ordered to be deported to a distant part of Russia. He had asked to be sent to Perm on the Volga, in the eastern part of European Russia, where he hoped that the Governor, who had known him as a youth at St. Petersburg, might befriend him. His wish was granted, and Evelina was allowed to accompany him with her child, on condition that she was subject to the same discipline.

While they were *en route* for Perm, orders arrived for the destination to be changed to Vologda in Northern Russia. During the last stage towards Moscow, the child Joseph became seriously ill. The escort refused to break the journey, and his life was only saved by the arrival of a doctor, an old friend of Apollo's, who rode out from Moscow to meet them, and persuaded the guard to see reason. Later still, Evelina herself became so weak that the soldiers were obliged to carry her, and an officer who met them on the outskirts of Nijni Novgorod was so shocked by the way the prisoners were treated that he obtained permission from headquarters for the young wife to rest in the city for some days.

The Governor of Vologda was an officer of humanity, treating his small band of Polish prisoners with a gentleness which did not match the climate. This was most severe, and was the cause of much suffering to people already defeated, humiliated, and bereaved. In addition to this, the Korzeniowskis had practically no money, and were only kept from starvation by Casimir Bobrowski who, unknown to the rest of his family, sent his brother-in-law what little he could.

During the summer of 1863 they were allowed, in consideration of Evelina's health, to leave Vologda for Tchernikow, which was further south and nearer their own province. Evelina herself obtained three months' leave, and with her little boy left for Nowofastow, in the Polish Ukraine, where her brother Thaddens had a property. Friends and relations came from near and far to show their appreciation of her devotion and suffering, but her health was shattered, and her only hope would have been to have stayed longer in a warm climate. Permission was flatly refused, and Conrad's brief glimpse of wider family life was ended. His mother lingered on until April 1865. She died at Tchernikow, of consumption, to which was added, in the words of Apollo, 'home-sickness, and the repeated blows which have fallen on our family.'

For the four years remaining to him, Apollo devoted much of his diminished energy to the composition of his memoirs, which, like his hopes and dreams, did not survive him. He did his best to educate his son. 'The poor child,' he wrote to a friend, 'does not know what it is to have a companion of his own age. He sees the sadness of my old age, and who knows, perhaps that sight may freeze and wither his own young heart.' In May 1866 he made up his mind to part with Conrad, and sent him to his cousins at Nowofastow. But Conrad seems to have pined for his father's society. 'We are both of us unhappy,' wrote Apollo soon after wards. 'The child is silly enough to be troubled about my solitude and to regret a life in whuch my gloomy face and his lessons have been his only distractions. . . . He languishes because he is a little fool. I am afraid he will always be one. He has grown, his face has changed, he begins to resemble his mother. May God bless him, for I, alas, cannot and never shall be able to do anything for him.'

While Conrad was at Nowofastow, Prince Roman Sanguzko, the hero of his one and only Polish story, came to see his uncle. He had been a comrade-in-arms of Apollo's father in the insurrection of 1831. He had been sentenced to Siberia for life, and had actually survived service in the mines. He was then allowed to enlist as a private soldier in the Caucasus, and returned to Poland fourteen years later completely deaf, but firm in resolve to devote the remnant of his strength and fortune to help his compatriots. To Conrad he remained always a half-legendary figure, symbol of his country's suffering.

Conrad spent the spring and summer of 1867 at Nowofastow, and in the autumn went to stay with his

grandmother at Jitomir. Meanwhile, as Apollo's strength
ebbed, his confinement was eased. The Russian Minister
of the Interior gave him a passport to go 'accompanied
by his son, ten years old, to Algiers and Madeira.'
Apollo was not well enough to travel so far, and it was
left to Joseph, in later, happier years, to gain acquaintance
with the Mediterranean. Lemberg in Galicia was the
immediate place decided on. Here Conrad was sent to
the Polish High School, though the teaching was not
wholly to his father's taste.

Galicia was under Austrian suzerainty. Of the three
powers which had swallowed Poland, Austria had always
shown most understanding to her people, and an evident
intention to conciliate them. Throughout Conrad's life,
while his hatred for Russia was unquenchable, and his
dislike for Germany, particularly in his later years, little
less strong, his feeling towards Austria was otherwise.
In the later sixties, while the persecution of the Poles
by the Russians and Prussians was unceasing, Austria's
attitude perceptibly softened. She herself had known
defeat, at Sadowa: she remembered, perhaps, Sobieski's
feats on her behalf in the days of Poland's pride, and
shortly after Apollo's arrival she allowed relative auto-
nomy to Galicia. Galician Poles could speak their
language freely and rejoiced in the concession.

Although the young Conrad was proving a delicate
child, his spirits now at last showed some revival.
Lemberg seems to have agreed with him, and even Apollo
brought himself to a more cheerful frame of mind. He
took his son away from school, so that he could himself
give him lessons, and 'see that his Polish is not changed
into the Galician language.'

At the beginning of 1869, father and son went to live
at Cracow, where the boy was again sent to school. At

Cracow, Apollo's last illness occurred. Many years later Conrad said of this time: 'I was a reading boy . . . I read! What did I not read!' Sometimes, he recalled, 'I would be permitted to tiptoe into the sick-room to say good-night to the figure prone on the bed, which could not acknowledge my presence but by a slow movement of the eyes, put my lips dutifully to the nerveless hand lying on the coverlet, and tiptoe out again. Then I would go to bed, in a room at the end of the corridor, and often, not always, cry myself into a good sound sleep.'

The end came in May. One evening Apollo, propped up in bed, supervised the burning af all his recent manuscripts. It was, as M. Jean-Aubry comments, 'the last act of renouncement on the part of one who was not only desperately ill, mortally weary, but a vanquished man.' He died on 23 May 1869. Although he had been but a short time in Cracow, his work for the Polish cause was widely known, and the funeral was impressive. People came, recorded Conrad many years later, 'to render homage to the ardent fidelity of the man whose life had been a fearless confession in word and deed of a creed which the simplest heart in that crowd could feel and understand.'

II

Conrad was then eleven. He continued living at Cracow, and had lessons at the St. Anne High School. He was backward in certain subjects, but worked hard, as he generally did. His grandmother took him on a short visit to Wartenberg in Bohemia and, when the autumn term began, returned with him to Cracow. She, together with Count Ladislas Mniszek, had become his

guardian, while a young tutor called Pulman, a student
at the University, looked after his studies, continuing to
do so for the next four years.

In 1872, in honour of his father, the Municipal
Council of Cracow gave him the freedom of the city.
This should have entailed naturalization as an Austrian
subject, but proceedings, though begun to this end,
were not concluded, probably owing to difficulties with
the Russian authorities. 'Since he could not be legally
what he was in fact,' says M. Jean-Aubry, 'anything was
better than being a Russian.'

As early as his fifteenth year, he confided to his uncle
Thaddeus a wish which was already apparently some years
old; it was—to go to sea. To Thaddeus it was a whim,
a typical Korzeniowski eccentricity. All the same, he
thought it worth while to travel from the Ukraine to
discuss the matter with the boy, and never met him
with a definite refusal. Conrad was, however, now
doing so well in his lessons that Pulman was in-
structed merely to discourage him as much as possible. Thaddeus hoped that a new and more reasonable
craze would develop.

In May 1873, on doctor's advice, boy and tutor made
a trip of about three months to Germany and Switzerland.
They visited Vienna, Munich and Schaffhausen. They
visited the Swiss Lakes, and went through the valley of
the Reuss by way of Andermatt and Hospenthal, crossing
the Furka Pass. It was on this journey that Conrad
decided, once for all, that there was only one career
possible for him. On this journey, too, he saw his
'unforgettable Englishman.' He described him in
A Personal Record as 'clad in a knickerbocker suit, but as
at the same time he wore socks under his laced boots,
for reasons which, whether hygienic or conscientious

were surely imaginative, his calves, exposed to the public gaze and to the tonic air of high altitudes, dazzled the beholder by the splendour of their marble-like condition and their rich tone of young ivory. He was the leader of a small caravan. The light of a headlong, exalted satisfaction with the world of men and the scenery of mountains illuminated his clean-cut, very red face, his short silver-white whiskers, his innocently eager and triumphant eyes.'

Conrad had indeed seen his Englishman. Shortly afterwards, visiting Venice and the Lido, he caught his first glimpse of the sea.

In July tutor and pupil returned to Cracow, where a final concerted effort was made by the family to dissuade Conrad from his fixed intention. So forceful was the battery that Conrad says, again in *A Personal Record*: 'I catch myself in times of solitude and retrospect meeting arguments and charges made thirty-five years ago by voices now for ever still; finding things to say that an assailed boy could not have found, simply because of the mysteriousness of his impulses to himself. I understood no more than the people who called upon me to explain myself.'

One other consideration may have had a part in strengthening his determination to seek adventure abroad. There is a passage in the Author's Note to *Nostromo* hinting that Antonia, a principal character in his most ambitious novel, is based on his first love. As is the way of such things, his feelings ran deep and, as they were certain of disappointment, a change of surroundings, from being desirable, seemed to have become imperative. He spent September 1874 with his cousins Antoine and Leon Syroczynski at Lemberg, and his grandmother and uncle Thaddeus arrived in October to accompany him back to Cracow. On the 14th they said farewell, and Conrad, in his own words, 'got into a train . . . on my way to the sea, as a man might go into a dream.' The prelude was over; the play about to begin, and it would open at Marseilles.

Conrad's had been a singular childhood, wholly starved of gaiety though never, mercifully, of love. Escape was as natural as it was necessary. His parents were dead; his country appeared so. Writers have written ingeniously upon the theory that, subconsciously, he realized, when leaving Poland, he was deserting the cause for which his family had lived and suffered. It may be so; but for a youth with the vitality and will which he possessed, no course could have been more natural. It was his choice of direction which was so unexpected. Although he had encountered his Englishman and beheld the Adriatic, it was to France that he first turned for adventure. She gave it him without stint.

FRANCE

THE traditional link between France and Poland was strong. It used to be said that, between the thirties and the sixties of the last century (the decades of smouldering insurrection), the spiritual capital of Poland was Paris. Almost all educated Poles had ties there; and to one starting a maritime career France and Austria offered by far the best possibilities. Russia was ruled out; so was Germany. They were both enemies and land powers. One of Conrad's most scornful asides occurs in the story 'Falk,' in which he remarks that the Germans call their master-mariners Schiff-fuhrers, which he rendered 'ship conductors.' It is indeed a source of continued surprise to sailors with a proper regard for their calling that in war an efficient Teuton mariner still calls himself 'a soldier of the Fatherland.' As for Austria, although during Conrad's youth some compatriots were rising to responsible posts at the Naval School at Pola, and although the Austrian service held possibilities of distinction, it came a long way second to that of France. Just as Conrad had failed to achieve Austrian nationality while at Cracow, so the idea of a regular career under the Austrian flag did not come within the immediate range of his ambition. His intention was to escape further. He had already, at Venice, had his imagination stirred by the means through which it could be achieved, and the whole world was before him.

Conrad's family had put themselves in touch with a Pole called Victor Chodso who had himself entered the French mercantile marine; he was one of the rare fellow-countrymen within whose orbit Conrad's sea experience led him. When Conrad arrived at Marseilles by way of Vienna, Geneva and Lyons, Chodso was away, but he had left him a message to get in touch with a man named Baptism Solary, who had promised to 'put Conrad in the way of getting a decent ship,' that is, if he really wanted a taste of what Solary called 'ce métier de chien.' But, charming as he was, Conrad says of him in *A Personal Record*, 'I fear he did not enter upon the quest of a ship for me in a very solemn spirit.' Solary had in fact gone ashore to seek a better livelihood with less risk. Conrad would in due course have his own thoughts on this very question: meanwhile, there were Solary's friends to meet, shipbrokers, master stevedores, shipwrights, above all, pilots. 'The very first whole day I ever spent on salt water,' he wrote in *A Personal Record*, 'was by invitation, in a big half-decked pilot-cutter, cruising under close-reefs on the look-out, in misty, blowing weather, for the sails of ships and the smoke of steamers rising out there, beyond the slim and tall Planier lighthouse cutting the line of the wind-swept horizon with a white perpendicular stroke.'

He seems never to have forgotten the smallest detail of visual experience. Many years later, in his last completed novel, *The Rover*, he was able to evoke the scenes of his French youth with precision and feeling.

'Under the general designation of *le petit ami de Baptistin*,' he says, 'I was made the guest of the Corporation of Pilots, and had the freedom of their boats night and day. . . . The first operation of seamanship I had an opportunity of observing was the boarding of ships at sea, at all times, in all states of the weather.' This was the more attractive side of his life at Marseilles; but there was another. He had the opportunity of acquaintance with royalist circles, and for a time became involved in them.

In 1875 the French Republic was young. The reign of Napoleon III had in effect ended with the resounding disaster of Sedan, but France had for centuries been used to crowns, and there were many, particularly in the conservative south, who built hopes upon a change of régime. Accident helped Conrad to realize this fact; for his uncle Thaddeus had opened a small account in Conrad's name, and the banker to whom he was accredited, M. Delestang, had a double claim upon him since he was also a ship-owner. Banking and shipping gained him his bread, but his passion lay elsewhere: he was a 'légitimiste'; 'such a frozen, mummified Royalist,' said Conrad later, 'that he used in current conversation terms of speech contemporary with the good Henry IV.' He even counted in écus instead of francs.

Mme Delestang, who reminded Conrad of Lady Dedlock in *Bleak House*, was an imposing woman. She held salons which he attended, though with increasing reluctance. Of the two societies he was beginning to know, he much preferred that of the Vieux-Port; yet it was to the Rue d'Arcole, where stood the Delestang offices, that he owed his early voyages.

The banker owned two vessels, the *Mont Blanc*, a ship of just under four hundred tons, and at that time over twenty years old, and the schooner *Saint Antoine*, which was newer. Conrad served in both; and although the exact chronology of this early period is uncertain, he probably spent Christmas 1874 aboard the *Mont Blanc*, 'running before a Gulf of Lyons gale, which made the old ship groan in every timber.' If this is indeed the ship referred to in the passage quoted from *The Mirror of the Sea*, she leaked. 'She leaked fully, generously, overflowingly, all over—like a basket.'

Leaky or not, it was in this same vessel, under the command of Captain Duteil, that Conrad set sail from Marseilles on 25 June 1875 on his first long voyage, doing the work of an ordinary seaman. The *Mont Blanc* was bound for St. Pierre, Martinique, and she arrived in the West Indies after a voyage of just over a month. She remained there two months, touched at St. Thomas at the end of September, and at Cap-Haitien loaded a cargo of log-wood for Le Havre. There, on Christmas Eve, 1875, Conrad landed, after a voyage of some six months. The ship had a stormy passage home, and received some damage. Conrad first listened in the *Mont Blanc* 'to the song of the wind in a ship's rigging' and the fact that she was old, small and difficult to handle would, on a long voyage, have tested his enthusiasm for his chosen calling.

As it was necessary for the *Mont Blanc* to be repaired at Le Havre, Conrad returned by train to Marseilles, breaking his journey for a few days in Paris. The Delestang's second ship was then at Martinique, and he decided to await her return before making plans for a further voyage. She arrived in May, and as her next cargo would not be ready until July, Conrad had six months of idleness. Not unnaturally, he fell into financial difficulties. He behaved, in fact, very much like any other youth after a trying voyage; made friends and enemies, got into scrapes, and in every way disturbed his affectionate but timid uncle Thaddeus, who, now as so often, came to his rescue. One story surviving from this time concerns an evening spent with some cleaned-out gamblers. Being unable to pay for their dinner, they sent young Conrad, who had never gambled before, to stake their last five francs. He returned with money for the bill, for a handsome tip for the waiter, and with a small balance to continue the party. There is no evidence that he ever tested his gambler's luck again, proof perhaps of his sense as well as of his innate pessimism.

On 10 July 1876 he set sail a second time for the West Indies. Captain Escarras commanded the *Saint Antoine*, and the crew consisted of four officers and thirteen men. For this trip Conrad was nominally rated as a steward, though it is improbable that he served as such; and in a later certificate he is referred to as a 'lieutenant.' However he appeared on the ship's books, he was in fact continuing to learn his trade. There were two shipmates of about his own age in the *Saint Antoine*, one of them being César Cervoni, a Corsican, the nephew of that Dominic Cervoni who appears in person in *The Mirror of the Sea*, and who served some five and twenty years afloat, partly in merchantmen, partly in the French Navy. 'His long experience,' says M. Jean-Aubry, 'the concentrated steadiness of his character, and his quick judgment, awoke in Conrad an admiration and affection which time never effaced.' He was humane, without illusions, with 'a contempt for the law, an ardent, romantic scepticism and a love of adventure which found an echo in the restless heart of his pupil.'

The *Saint Antoine* took thirty-nine days to St. Pierre, where she remained for just over a month. Then, like the *Mont Blanc*, she headed for St. Thomas. Fifteen days later, she loaded at Port-au-Prince with logwood and sugar for Marseilles. She had returned to France by 15 February 1877.

Logwood and sugar may have been her nominal bill-of-lading; actually the ship was engaged in illicit arms traffic. She carried munitions for one of the political parties in a Central American republic. Conrad spoke later of 'a four days' passage between two places in the Gulf of Mexico whose names don't matter,' undergone in a 'small and very dirty little schooner' which was undoubtedly his second ship. On these early voyages, he imbibed the atmosphere reproduced in *Romance*, the second and better of his collaborations with Ford Madox Ford, and more particularly in *Nostromo*.

Having made two West Indies voyages, one in each of their ships, Conrad then quarrelled with the Delestangs, and soon involved his affairs with those of a group of Carlists, sympathizers with the claimant to the throne of Spain, Don Carlos. It was a new manifestation of a familiar subject, royalism. With other young men, he formed a syndicate to buy a sixty-ton tartane, the *Tremolino*, which was to be in charge of his friend Dominic Cervoni, and to run arms in the claimant's cause. Although it was adventure with which Conrad was really in love, no one appears to have doubted his devotion to the Cause, and its service led him to a series of risky voyages between Marseilles and the Spanish coast. These are referred to in a well-known chapter of *The Mirror of the Sea* and, less satisfactorily though with undoubted feeling, in one of his later novels, *The Arrow of Gold*. The adventure, doomed to failure, ended when the little ship was driven against the rocks of the Baie de Rosas, in order to escape the Spanish coastguards.

'All this gun-running,' wrote Conrad many years afterwards in a letter to Sir John Squire, 'was a very dull if dangerous business. As to intrigues, if there were any, I didn't know anything of them. But in truth, the Carlist invasion was a very straightforward adventure conducted with inconceivable stupidity and a foredoomed failure from the first.'

At this time another shadowy figure entered into Conrad's life, the girl Rita, heroine of *The Arrow of Gold*. The course of his affair appears to have been mysterious, exciting and unsatisfactory. Rita, if that was her name, is said to have attracted Don Carlos himself, and to have been the mistress of a rich Parisian who had left her a large fortune, which she devoted to the claimant. Conrad felt for Rita passionately, but their relationship, which on Rita's side is unlikely to have been serious, ended suddenly and dramatically. Conrad fought a duel about her with an American, J. M. K. Blunt, in which he received a bullet wound. Thaddeus was notified in a telegram sent in the later part of February 1878, and hurriedly left Kiev for Marseilles.

He found his nephew on his feet, physically, but destitute of other means of support. Thaddeus remained a fortnight, long enough to assure himself that Conrad had come to no lasting harm. He helped Conrad in his decision to leave Marseilles, which now seemed almost intolerable to him. In the previous year he had considered taking French nationality, but had been persuaded against this course by Thaddeus, 'on account of obligatory military service.' He now took the second most momentous step in his life. On 24 April 1878 he joined the English steamer *Mavis*, bound for Constantinople with a cargo of coal.

The Russo-Turkish war was then just over, the Russians victorious. The British fleet had been sent to Constantinople with the intention of checking their further progress westwards. Years later Conrad recorded 'as we went up the Bosphorus we saw the tents of the Russian Army at San Stephano.' His sense of security, derived from being in a ship wearing the red ensign, was heightened by the presence of the white ensign in the Golden Horn.

The *Mavis* next proceeded to Yeisk, at the extremity of the Sea of Azov, where she loaded linseed consigned to Lowestoft. At Lowestoft, on 18 June 1878, Conrad first set foot upon English soil.

THE RED ENSIGN

I

IT was high summer, and Conrad was young. But he was alone, knew scarcely any English, and had no friends ashore. His money was low; France was, at the time, an unfortunate memory; above all, he felt that even his faithful uncle was still annoyed at his escapades. That he was right in this respect was proved soon enough, for shortly after he landed he received a letter from Thaddeus bidding him work hard and live within his means. Thaddeus added that he himself had not been able to go to Marienbad that year, through having to pay for his nephew's follies. He ended: 'You wanted to be a sailor, and you must be responsible for the consequences; you have forfeited my confidence. Work now to regain it; you will win it back if you apply yourself steadily and pull yourself together.'

Such avuncularity, however deserved, would have caused many youths to tear up the letter in impatience, curse their luck, and go on a bust with the last of their money. With Conrad it had exactly the effect intended, for he was devoted to Thaddeus, and must have been softened considerably by what followed. 'If you cannot find a ship for the monent,' continued the letter, 'take to something—shop-keeping or anything else, but work.' He added that he was arranging for 600 francs to be sent to him. 'Live as you can on that money,' said Thaddeus, 'and if at present you cannot pay your premium' (as an apprentice officer) 'enroll yourself as an Able-Bodied

Seaman. If you learn what poverty is, that will teach you to value the money given you by others. . . . I do not want to work for a lazy fellow.'

There was at this time some talk of Conrad joining the French Navy: one biographer, Ford Madox Ford (who should have known better) said indeed that he did so. In fact, it would have required naturalization, and nothing came of it. But he was to be spared another dangerous period without work. On 11 July 1878 he returned to sail, always his real love. He signed on in a coastal barquentine, the *Skimmer of the Seas*, which plied between Lowestoft and Newcastle-on-Tyne. In a little over two months he had made several voyages between these places, and his English, which he was learning the hard way, increased daily. He read, he studied navigation, and he liked his fellow-seamen. Years later, the *Skimmer* was lost with many good hands; later still, Conrad wrote to his friend Cunninghame Graham: 'In that craft I began to learn English from East Coast chaps, each built as though to last for ever, and coloured like a Christmas card. Tan and pink—gold hair and blue eyes —with that Northern straight-away-there look! . . . From Lowestoft to Newcastle and back again. Good school for a seaman.'

Conrad was in luck, and appreciated it with discernment beyond his years. He had already experienced both deep-water seafaring and the life of the coast; he was therefore in a position, none better, to assess the dangers and skills of the English coastal trade. In *Notes on Life and Letters* he referred to his sea-teachers as 'sailors of the Norfolk shore: coast men, with steady eyes, mighty limbs, and gentle voice; men of very few words, which at least were never bare of meaning. Honest, strong, steady men, sobered by domestic ties.' The affinities of these 'East Coast chaps' were with Holland, Flanders and the northern kingdoms, and within their particular limits there were, and are, no better seamen.

The coast-wise trade was, however, a school, not a profession. Conrad intended to see the world at large, and found an opportunity through reading the *Standard* newspaper, from which he was acquiring written English. He saw the advertisement of a firm of shipping agents in its columns. To them he wrote his first letter in our language, following it up within a few days by a visit in person to the offices in London. 'No explorer could have been more lonely,' he recorded in *Notes on Life and Letters*. 'I did not know a single soul of all these millions that all around me peopled the mysterious distances of the streets. I had vowed to myself not to inquire my way from anyone. Youth is the time of easy pledges. Had I taken a wrong turning I would have been lost; and if faithful to my pledge I might have remained lost for weeks, have left, perhaps, my bones to be discovered bleaching in some blind alley of the Whitechapel district, as it has happened to lonely travellers lost in the Bush. But I walked on to my destination without hesitation or mistake, showing there, for the first time, some of that faculty to absorb and make my own, the imaged topography of a chart, which in later years was to help me in regions of intricate navigation to keep the ships entrusted to me off the ground.'

The shipping agents' office, when he reached it, was Dickensian. In one guise or another, it appears frequently in his fiction. Windows grey with the dust of decades hid from casual eyes a man with a big grey beard, and a head of white curly hair 'which gave him the look of an apostle in the Baroque Italian style.' On his nose were silver-rimmed spectacles and—final Dickensian touch—he was eating a chop, a process which was not interrupted as he explained that his proper business was finding ships for young men who wished to go to sea as premium apprentices.

Conrad had no money for such a venture. 'Of course,' said the man, 'I see you are a gentleman, but your wish is to get a berth before the mast as an Able-Seaman, if possible. Isn't that it?' Conrad agreed. Alas, an Act of Parliament stood in the way. It made it a penal offence to procure ships for seamen. ' "An Act of Parliament. A Law." He took pains to impress it again and again on my foreign understanding, while I looked at him in consternation,' wrote Conrad. 'I had not been half an hour in London before I had run my head against an Act of Parliament! What a hopeless adventure.'

Conrad had yet another lesson to learn on that momentous day: it was that even Acts of Parliament could be circumvented. Without a blush the apostle with the chop, seeing his distress, suggested that he might manage to get him a berth on 'a very fine wool clipper,' the *Duke of Sutherland*, which 'knew the round to the Antipodes better than her own skipper.' Conrad nodded, eager but bewildered, and on 15 October 1878 was actually embarked for Sydney.

His service on the *Duke of Sutherland* lasted just a year, and, so far as his biography is concerned, it is one almost empty of event. It is true that an incident in *The Mirror of the Sea* dates from this time, where he tells how he was knocked out one night by a fugitive from justice; but the long return voyage, though it added much to his experience, does not seem to have been agreeable. His still limited knowledge of English, the hard conditions before the mast, and the great fatigue of the work made this one round voyage his last in this ship.

Lack of nationality occupied much space in his letters at this time to his uncle. Thaddeus would have been content had he become English, French, Swiss or even Austrian. Until Conrad had regularized his position, Thaddeus discouraged him from visiting the Ukraine, to which he felt drawn, since his uncle knew that he could not return to Poland without risk from the Russian authorities. Meanwhile, his next ambition was to revisit old haunts in the Mediterranean, the former pain of association having now become dulled. In order to do so he found a berth in the steamship *Europa*. He embarked, on 12 December 1879, for Genoa, Leghorn, Naples, Patras, Cephalonia, Messina and Palermo. It was a short voyage, and he was back in England by the end of January. But once again he was unhappy. The captain had proved a difficult man to work for, and Conrad's health was indifferent. He landed with fever and a severe cough. He had practically no money, and for once his uncle (who was himself in difficulties) could do no more than give him advice. He sympathized with Conrad's troubles, and added, characteristically: 'I do not understand the way the English reason, but one cannot change them and one must adapt oneself to them.' This Conrad was in fact doing. His knowledge of the language was actually increasing so fast that he was already thinking of taking an examination for a third-mate's certificate, although it was scarcely eighteen months since he had begun to learn.

Conrad was fleetingly tempted to work as secretary to a Canadian business man. 'Is it sensible,' asked his uncle, 'to link your fate to a man—however great he may be—who is a business man or a politician? It is far more dignified and sensible to stick to a profession which one gets to understand more and more by working

at it. You have chosen to be a sailor . . . and I am sure
that you will succeed without constantly changing your
occupation.'

The advice was heeded. Conrad continued to study,
and in June 1880 he passed the examination he had
aimed at. 'That day,' says a character in his novel
Chance, 'I wouldn't have called the Queen my cousin.'
He had every reason to be proud of the result, achieved
in face of assessors of the Marine Board at the St.
Katherine's Dock House on Tower Hill. It was the
finest day of his life and, when his uncle heard his news,
he appreciated its full flavour. 'My dear boy and
lieutenant,' his congratulatory letter began, 'you have
filled me with joy. . . . You have proved to your uncle
and to the whole world that you have not eaten unearned
bread during these first years; you have been able to
overcome the drawbacks of being a foreigner without
backing. . . . I congratulate you, *Monsieur l'officier de
second rang de la Marine de la Grande-Bretagne.*'

Thaddeus did not exaggerate. It was a distinguished
feat, as any layman can appreciate by a single glance at
Conrad's principal tutor. This was Newton's *Guide for
Masters and Mates*; a formidable, packed, and wholly
practical vade-mecum for the aspiring seaman: a concise
technical education in itself. In its own way there is no
more impressive landmark in Conrad's life. The ordeal
itself was severe. Of the assessor, Conrad says, again in
Chance: 'He kept me for an hour and a half in the torture
chamber, and behaved as though he hated me. He kept
his eyes shaded with one of his hands. Suddenly he let
it drop saying, "You will do!" Before I realized what he
meant he was pushing the blue slip across the table.
I jumped up as if my chair had caught fire.'

It was not merely that a modest hurdle had been

taken: Conrad had now earned the right to serve as an officer; more important still, he had forced open the formidable door of the English language. Henceforward, he would use it with increasing assurance, and what he had now mastered would serve him as the groundwork for examinations to come. As for practical sea experience, his store was already growing considerable.

A little over two months later he received an officer's appointment to the *Loch Etive*, a sailing ship of 1,200 tons, registered at Glasgow. She was not yet three years old and was commanded by William Stuart of Peterhead, who had made a splendid reputation for fast passages in the clipper *Tweed*, one of the swiftest known.

The *Loch Etive* was a fine ship; Captain Stuart was to command her the rest of his life, to love her deeply, and to sail her as well as he could, though he never again approached the speed which had made him famous in the *Tweed*. Conrad was not only the youngest officer aboard; he had additional responsibility thrust on him through the sickness of the second mate, which did not make his relations with the captain, a man of uncertain temper, at all easy. The *Loch Etive* reached Sydney in November, and left again early in December for London by way of the Horn—'Cape Stiff,' the sternest test for the old-time shell-back, the grave of fine ships and men. She reached London in April, and Conrad left her on the 25th. 'You have proved this time,' wrote his uncle at the end of the voyage, 'that you are more mature than your years.' He was right; for the *Loch Etive*'s voyage had been inspiring as well as testing, and it had determined Conrad to try for his next step. It had also given him a lasting idea of the dignity of his chosen profession. His letters, says his uncle, breathe 'ardour and enterprise.' He approves, though he can no longer share these feelings. He even urges his nephew—whose Polish, he says, is still commendable—to contribute a series of letters about foreign places to a well known newspaper in Warsaw. 'Six letters a year from different countries will not take up much of your time. It would entertain you and others.' Thaddeus had a certain literary talent of his own, as is shown in his memoirs. He had the discernment to see a similar quality in his nephew. But at this time, Conrad did nothing. His profession in itself afforded sufficient occupation.

He had a spell in a ship called the *Anne Frost*, towards the middle of 1881. In her he had an accident, though of its nature nothing is now known. Thaddeus sent him £10 'as a distressed seaman.' Then, on 21 September 1881, he embarked on the adventure which he took for his very well-known story, *Youth*. He sailed as second mate in the *Palestine*, a small barque of 425 tons, London owned. She was old, like her captain, whose first command she was. She leaked like a sieve—leaked, in fact, like the *Mont Blanc*.

The bald facts were as follows. She sailed first from London to Yarmouth, taking more than a week over the passage. A fortnight later she was at Newcastle. Safely there, she required six weeks for repair; on 29 November 1881 she started hopefully for Bangkok with a crew of eight seamen and two boys, and a cargo of 500 tons of coal. In the Channel, the leaks sprung again, and the men refused to proceed on so long a journey with the ship in her condition. So she put into Falmouth, where her whole consignment, but for ninety tons, was discharged and stored under cover, while the ship was once more patched. Conrad, in the months that followed, idled, chafed and read Shakespeare.

Again they put to sea, but after a disastrous experience

with heavy weather, the crew again struck, the ship returned, and what appeared to be a proper repair in dry-dock was made, though again after long delay. She cleared the land at last on 17 September 1882, and had a good wind and a calm sea right into the tropics. Creeping slowly along, the old barque entered the Indian Ocean and then turned north towards Java Head. Suddenly, on 11 March, the cargo was discovered to be on fire. On the 13th some tons of coal were jettisoned. Next day, the deck blew up, and the vessel was abandoned. The boats stood by her until the early morning of the 15th, when the hull was a mass of flames. There then followed a boat journey which inspired the last pages of *Youth*. Finally, Conrad had his first sight of that Eastern world which he was to make so particularly his own.

When the crew reached Singapore, Conrad remained in that port for the whole of April, waiting for a chance to return to England. In May, he took passage in a steamer, and arrived at Liverpool in June, ready to sit for his second examination. An even more important step was in his mind. This was to obtain British citizenship, a procedure urged by his uncle, who said, 'It is your skin that is at stake.' What he meant was that, however they might wish it, the pair could not meet in safety on Polish soil until the matter was settled.

Conrad duly passed his examination in July, after 'forty minutes' torture.' He then set forth for Marienbad, where Thaddeus was taking the waters, and spent a full month there, and at Toplitz, near the Saxon frontier. The two had not seen each other for five years, and the meeting was in every way pleasurable. On Conrad's return to London, Thaddeus wrote: 'Everything you say I shall remember in my heart. I was sad and depressed when in the evening I sat down at table opposite your empty chair.'

On 10 September 1883 Conrad embarked as second mate in the ship *Riversdale*, bound for Madras. He had some sort of dispute with the captain, L. B. McDonald, who in his certificate of discharge declined to comment on his 'character for conduct' (the only instance of the kind in his career), though he rated his 'character for ability' very good. From Madras Conrad went to Bombay in search of new employment. He was offered it in a mail boat, but was reluctant to serve in steam. Instead, after waiting some little time, he saw a graceful ship, the *Narcissus*, of 1,300 tons, come sailing into the harbour. Soon afterwards, he joined her.

On 28 April 1884 the *Narcissus* sailed for Dunkirk, where she was later dismantled. She will always be famous, for she and her men served as the material for one of Conrad's best stories—*The Nigger of the 'Narcissus'*. It is one of which he himself was particularly fond, and it is a study, primarily, of life in the forecastle and of stress of weather. Conrad told M. Jean-Aubry that, apart from changes in detail and in the names of characters, 'the voyage of the *Narcissus* was performed from Bombay to London in the manner I have described.'

The winter of 1884 he spent in London. Thaddeus had made over to him the total of various small legacies and gifts he had accumulated on his nephew's behalf, a few hundred pounds which would give a modest reserve to fall back upon. On 24 April of the year following he left Hull as second mate of the 1,500 ton *Tilkhurst*, bound first for Cardiff and later for Singapore.

At Cardiff occurred one of his rare meetings with compatriots in exile. In the course of examination before the Board of Trade, an assessor had actually asked him if

D

he had ever met a Pole serving at sea. Conrad had; but only once. This man, Komorowski by name, had escaped Russian conscription by stowing away in a German ship. He had asked Conrad to execute a small commission for him, should he ever find himself at Cardiff.

The errand was with another Pole, Kliszczewski, a watchmaker. Conrad found his sympathies strongly aroused by this man, who had emigrated to England after the Insurrection of 1831. When he heard the Polish language spoken once more in his shop, Kliszczewski received the young officer with enthusiastic warmth, and a friendship began between Conrad, the watchmaker and his son Spiridion which lasted over many years. He wrote a series of letters to Spiridion, a young man of about his own age, beginning in the course of the voyage which followed.

During this time Conrad was considering the idea of gaining first-hand knowledge of whaling. The captain of the *Narcissus* had been a harpooner in Peterhead ships. 'When he spoke of that time,' wrote Conrad later, 'his restless grey eyes became still and cold, like the loom of ice. Afterwards he went into the East Indian trade for the sake of change.' As the *Tilkhurst* rolled on her way to Singapore, Conrad's thoughts dwelt upon past talks on the subject, and the prospects of the life his former captain had once enjoyed, but later abandoned. It was a fine voyage, memorable for a passage he wrote in a letter to Spiridion as to his feelings about England. 'I understand and readily accept your reference to "Home," ' he said. 'When speaking, writing or thinking in English, the word "home" always means for me the hospitable shores of Great Britain.'

From Singapore the *Tilkhurst* ran to Calcutta. There

Conrad recorded his immediate ambition, which was to pass his final examination. This would give him a Master Mariner's ticket. He felt quite confident. 'I was not frightened of being plucked,' he said later. 'The eventuality did not even present itself to my mind.' Whaling, his other cherished hope, held more difficulties. Although he had 'read, studied, pumped professional men and imbibed knowledge upon whale-fishing and sealing for the last four years,' he was doubtful whether he could raise the necessary funds, which he thought would need to be large. He asked Spiridion's advice, being then 'sick and tired of sailing about for little money and less consideration. But I love the sea: and if I could just clear my bare living in the way I suggested I should be comparatively happy. Can it be done?' He asked the question with all the more excitement since the ship was going 'actually to Dundee (next door to Peterhead).' Spiridion discouraged him; indeed he told M. Jean-Aubry many years later that in the end he had been able to dissuade him.

Meanwhile Conrad gave his new-found confidant a gloomy forecast of the prospects of the British Empire. His hopes had been pinned, about that time, to an Anglo-German alliance against Russia. This idea he saw dissolve. 'Joy reigns in St. Petersburg, no doubt,' he wrote: 'the International Socialist Association are triumphant, and every disreputable ragamuffin in Europe feels that the day of universal brotherhood, despoliation and disorder is coming apace.' He thought (in 1889) that the Empire had 'already gone over the edge . . . the sun is set and the last barrier removed. England was the only barrier to the pressure of infernal doctrines born in continental back-slums. Now, there is nothing! The destiny of this nation and of all nations is to be accomplished in darkness amidst much weeping and gnashing of teeth, to pass through robbery, equality, anarchy and misery under the iron rule of a militarism. . . . The whole herd of idiotic humanity are running in that direction at the bidding of unscrupulous rascals and a few sincere but dangerous lunatics. . . . Neither you nor I shall live to see the final crash: although we may both turn in our graves when it comes, for we both feel deeply and sincerely.'

This might have been taken as an outburst of youthful gloom, were it not based upon, in his own phrase, 'common-sense logic.' Conrad felt passionately about politics: loved order, loathed the forces of disintegration and felt them keenly around him. His words read more reasonably to-day, but they would have seemed odd, and rather mad, to most Englishmen of the time.

Whatever the depression caused by his wider-ranging thoughts, and his increasing concern about his health, his time in the *Tilkhurst* was otherwise happy. The voyage home was easy and pleasant, and the ship discharged at Dundee on 17 June 1886. He had grown attached to his captain, Blackie, and went south to London with him and his wife. He called him later 'the least sailor-like in outward appearance, but certainly one of the best seamen whom it has been my lot to serve under.' Although in fact never again able to go to sea, this kindly man said to Conrad on parting: 'If you happen to be in want of employment, remember that as long as I have a ship, you have a ship too.'

Before his next employment, there was at last to mature a proposal which had long been in abeyance—his naturalization. On 19 August 1886, Joseph Conrad Korzeniowski, 'subject of the Russian Empire, of the age of twenty-nine years, mariner, unmarried' obtained a certificate of British naturalization. As if this were not enough, three months later he obtained his 'Certificate of Competency as Master' in the British mercantile marine. He had now an official country, recognized professional status, and comprehensive experience of his chosen life. 'It was a fact, I said to myself, that I was now a British Master Mariner beyond a doubt. It was not that I had an exaggerated sense of my very modest achievement,' he wrote in *A Personal Record*, 'with which, however, luck, opportunity, or any extraneous influence could have nothing to do. The fact, satisfactory and obscure in itself, had for me a certain ideal significance. It was an answer to a certain outspoken scepticism and even to some not very kind aspersions. I had vindicated myself from what had been cried upon as a stupid obstinacy, or a fantastic caprice.'

The word ideal as used in this context by Conrad was true in a double sense, for there is no question that for him the British master mariner represented something more than a seaman of recognized competence. He was a symbol of order and authority in the world. These were two qualities which Conrad, in common with most sensible men, believed to be essential for right living. 'Having been the honourable provider of means to this achievement,' wrote Thaddeus, full of pride, 'I can only congratulate my pennies on not having been thrown away, but on having helped you to the top of the profession you chose. . . . You are twenty-nine and the ball is at your feet. Do whatever seems good to you.'

One of the first things Conrad did was to write a story, 'The Black Mate,' his first and almost his last in a vein of comedy. It was unsuccessful in the competition for which it was submitted. There is no indication that he was affected by disappointment, or indeed that he attached any particular importance to the matter.

II

Even a British master mariner could not live on reputation and a certificate. Thaddeus was increasingly pressed by other family cares, and Conrad's Polish money, all his normal expectations now gathered in, was earning but a tiny income in the care of Barr, Moering and Co., into whose hands he had placed it. One of the firm's directors, Adolf Kreiger by name, was a close friend; the nature of his business, transport. The income so derived was useful as a supplement to regular earnings, but could not support him.

On 16 February 1887, he took a post as Chief Officer, or as it was called in a sailing ship, first mate, in the Glasgow *Highland Forest*. She was then at Amsterdam, bound ultimately for Samarang in Java.

A fine chapter in *The Mirror of the Sea* describes the Dutch winter with the shrewd detail of a Cuyp: the waiting, the uncertainty, the friendliness of the agents, his feeling of responsibility as executive officer, in charge of all the ship's affairs until the arrival of the master. He had the theory of stowage at his finger-tips, just like any good examinee: what he had yet to learn was that each ship handles differently, and that he had not got the trick of the *Highland Forest*. They later rolled their way across the ocean with indescribable discomfort, and although the master, when he did appear, was a man of parts, and was in fact no other than the John McWhirr who became the hero of *Typhoon* (in which story he had command of a steamer), 'the voyage,' in Conrad's phrase, 'was lively but not joyful.'

As if to pay him out for professional error, the ship, towards the end of the passage, took revenge on her hapless mate. 'It was a wonder,' said Conrad, 'the men sent aloft were not flung off the yards, the yards not flung off the masts, the masts not flung overboard.' One 'piece of minor spar' did in fact come unshipped; it struck Conrad in the small of the back, and knocked him down. He reported to the doctor in Samarang as having 'inexplicable periods of powerlessness, sudden accesses of mysterious pain.' The doctor was anxious for him to take his discharge, which he did on 18 July, proceeding at once to Singapore, and staying in hospital for some weeks. While there, he enjoyed the peaceful warmth of the tropics, and thought without relish of the bitter days of the early part of the year.

He now sought relief from the rigours of sail, and took what was for him an easy berth. He joined the small steamship *Vidar* (800 tons) as mate. Her voyages were short, and confined to local seas. The work proved as light as he had expected. Through her he came to know the coasts of Malaya as few have known them—to soak them into his very being. His immediate impression was one of contrast. For years he had known the turbulence of the great oceans. Now his traffic was in sunlit seas, and among races which, like his own, had been defeated, but had retained their pride. The Dutch, the English and the Arab had spread over and exploited Malaya, but to Conrad it was the vanquished rather than the newcomers who were exciting, sympathetic, and sometimes fascinating.

ENCHANTMENT AND OTHERWISE

I

READING steadily through Conrad's fiction, an impression that he had spent years among the Spice Islands of the Malay Archipelago is almost inevitable. This was not so. His close acquaintance with those shores was actually measured in months, though, from the point of view of literary material, they were the most profitable of his life.

The *Vidar* was owned by an Arab, and sailed under the Dutch flag, though with an English master. Conrad's portraits of Dutchmen in the Far East are as a whole unflattering, quite the opposite of his rare cameos of the men of Holland. He liked the little he knew of the 'excellent (and picturesque) Arab owner, about whom one needed not to trouble,' and he liked his shipmates, particularly his captain, who said of him many years afterwards: 'He pleased me at once by his manners, which were distinguished and reserved; one of the first things he told me was that he was a foreigner by birth, which I had already guessed from his accent.'

The ship was managed by this same captain. Her complement included two European engineers, and one Chinese; Conrad and one other mate, Mahamat; eleven Malays, and eighty-two Chinamen who were used for loading and unloading gum and resin. The regular run of the *Vidar* was as follows: Singapore, through the Karimata Strait into the Java Sea to Banjermassim in South Borneo; thence to the islet of Laut, which lies south-east of the main island. There she coaled. She ran between Laut and Borneo northwards, then north-east to Dongala in Celebes: from there to Bulungan on the east coast of Borneo; thence she returned to Singapore.

The small places visited were mostly at the mouths of tortuous and little-known rivers. They consisted of one long street, and the banks of the estuaries were thick with vegetation. This is the setting of many of Conrad's stories. In all, he made just five such journeys—between August 1887 and January 1888; not a long time in which to have absorbed so much, and to have met the originals of Tom Lingard, Almayer, Willems, Captain Whalley, not to speak of the many Dutch, Arab and Malayan characters who people his works.

The master was a mine of information about the islands, which he had known for many years. The work itself was light, and although Conrad's flat statement that he never in his life made a note of any kind has already been referred to, the captain recalled years later that, whenever he went down to the cabin to talk to his mate, he found him writing.

Almayer, the principal character of his first two books, *Almayer's Folly* and *An Outcast of the Islands*, was in fact a derelict Dutchman who lived at Bulungan, much as he is described; a man in whom actual dilapidation is contrasted with the vastness of his ambition. He made a deep impression on Conrad, who said later: 'If I had not got to know Almayer pretty well, it is almost certain there would never have been a line of mine in print.' Almayer had married a Malayan woman, and died of a wound received on a python-hunt.

As for Tom Lingard, he was captain of a schooner trading, like the *Vidar*, in those enchanted seas. Jim, the hero of *Lord Jim*, was actually Lingard's nephew, his nickname, 'Lord,' a translation of the Malay 'Tuan.' It derived from 'the swaggering manner he assumed, when meeting our ship,' so Conrad's captain later told his biographer.

Conrad's spell in the *Vidar* served a double purpose. It restored his health, and set his imagination working. These were, in fact, vital months in his life, for, if they did not actually incline him to write, they at least determined him in what he should write about, if ever the choice were made. He was never happier. Years later he wrote: 'It is part of my sea life to which my memory returns most often, since there is nothing to remember but what is good and pleasant.'

It was Conrad's nature to be restless. Pleasure was something to be accepted, but never to satisfy. Existence in the *Vidar* (to quote from a story) 'was not a very enterprising life for a man who had served famous firms, who had sailed famous ships.' 'One goes on,' he says elsewhere, 'and the time, too, goes on, till one perceives ahead a shadow line warning one that the region of early youth, too, must be left behind.' He became disenchanted; threw up his congenial job, and at Singapore, quite unexpectedly, received his first command, the circumstances of which are related in faithful detail in more than one of his stories.

She was the barque *Otago*. She herself survived until lately, though long used as a coal hulk at Hobart, and her wheel is preserved in London, in the sloop *Wellington* moored in the Thames. She then lay at Bangkok, to which place the ill-fated *Palestine* had once been bound. Conrad was ordered to take her to Melbourne.

He found the ship haunted. First there was the master from whom he had inherited command; a man who, apparently, had wished all on board to perish, a mad, fiddle-playing irresponsible who would scarcely be credited in a novel. The mate, good seaman as he had once been, was soured with disappointment at not taking the place of the late captain. He was, in fact, a little daft. The second mate was useless; the crew were sick almost to a man, and although the ship herself was 'a creature of high breed' (in Conrad's words) she appeared to be stuck in the port, her affairs disordered, an air of decay surrounding her. In all the stories relating to this time—'Falk,' 'The Secret Sharer,' 'The Shadow Line'—the atmosphere is consistent, but it is not cheerful.

The former captain's interests appear to have been confined to wild music and to writing indecent poems in account books in which no reasonable figures could ever be made out. No method could be discerned even in his lunacy. It transpired that he told his owners nothing. There were few stores on board; a Chinaman absconded with Conrad's small supply of ready money; the cargo was accumulating with painful slowness, and in fact it was by a miracle of will-power that Conrad got the ship to sail at all. Even then, she seemed to be dogged by the ghost of her former captain throughout her slow progress down the Gulf of Siam.

Conrad's reactions to this prolonged crisis was characteristic. He was proud of his command; he was determined to break the evil spell which seemed to encoil her; and, once clear of Bangkok, while possessing the proper sense of responsibility which should belong to any senior officer, he was prepared to take what seemed to his officers the most remarkable risks at sea. This was not recklessness so much as a wish to pit his wits, experience and luck against the elements and the natural dangers of navigation. It added spice to life and helped to appease that restless curiosity which was an essential part of his nature.

The two men who helped him most to leave Bangkok were a certain Doctor Willis who, unasked, recorded in writing his admiration of Conrad's efforts to fight disease and save the lives of those in his care, and his cook, a first-rate sailor who was occupied in an unfamiliar role owing to a weak heart. He and Conrad were virtually the only active seamen on board, for the mate succumbed to sickness and became nothing more than a passenger. As a last detail of horror, when the barque did in the end get away, Conrad discovered that the vital stock of quinine on board had been squandered by his predecessor, and the bottles filled up with some useless substance whose look had deceived both himself and the friendly doctor.

The *Otago* took three weeks over the eight-hundred-mile passage to Singapore. She arrived there more like a derelict than an active vessel. But the worst was over. By resolution Conrad had surmounted his difficulties, while he had always known that the ship herself, once she had an efficient crew, was all he could have wished. Moreover, his owners, Henry Simpson and Sons of Adelaide, could scarcely have proved easier. They were no doubt surprised, perhaps a little incredulous, at the skill, efficiency and loyalty of their new captain, with the strange name of Korzeniowski.

The barque left Singapore for Sydney in March 1888, reaching her destination in May. Thence she proceeded to Melbourne, Adelaide, Sydney once more, and then away to Mauritius. At Adelaide, Conrad had suggested to the owners that the *Otago* should sail by way of the dangerous Torres Strait between Australia and New Guinea; this despite the fact that this route was so rarely used by sailing vessels that an additional insurance premium was required. The owners paid this without demur.

'It was not without a certain emotion,' he wrote in

the last year of his life (in 'Geography and Some Explorers'), 'that, commanding very likely the first, and certainly the last merchant ship that carried a cargo that way—from Sydney to Mauritius—I put her head at daybreak for Bligh's Entrance, and packed on her every bit of canvas she could carry. Wind-swept, sunlit, empty waters were all around me, half-veiled by a brilliant haze. The first thing that caught my eyes upon the play of green white-capped waves was a black speck marking conveniently the end of a low sand-bank. It looked like the wreck of some small vessel.

'I altered the course slightly in order to pass close, with the hope of being able to read the letters on her stern. They were already faded. Her name was *Honolulu*. The name of the port I could not make out. The story of her life is known by now to God alone, and the winds must have drifted long ago around her remains a quiet grave of the very sand on which she had died. Thirty-six hours afterwards, of which about nine were spent at anchor, approaching the other end of the strait, I sighted a gaunt, grey wreck of an American ship lying high and dry on the southernmost of the Warrior Reefs. She had been there for years. I had heard of her. She was legendary. She loomed up, a sinister and enormous *memento mori* raised by the refraction of this serene afternoon above the far-away line of the horizon drawn under the sinking sun.

'And thus I passed out of the Torres Strait before the dusk settled on its waters. Just as a clear sun sank ahead of my ship I took a bearing of a little island for a fresh departure, an insignificant crumb of dark earth, lonely, like an advanced sentinel of that mass of broken land and water, to watch the approaches from the side of the Arafura Sea.'

Characteristic of Conrad was risk without mishap. The *Otago* reached Mauritius safely, and returned thence to Adelaide. There he found a letter waiting for him from his uncle, who was concerned lest there should have been any hitch in his British naturalization. Conrad seems for once to have neglected to keep Thaddeus fully informed of his affairs, and his uncle now inquired anxiously if 'the formality in excusing allegiance to the Tsar is an accomplished fact? . . . Perhaps it is all settled. In that case, we can hope to see each other in the country.'

There were other indications that Thaddeus was uneasy. He had made arrangements for the disposition of his property, and it is probable that it was the state of his uncle's mind and health, news of which would have reached Conrad as he took the *Otago* between Adelaide, Melbourne and Sydney, that decided him to resign command. There were, of course, other factors. Of these, his own restlessness was again the chief, and a longing which had come over him to return once more to Europe.

In April 1889 a letter from Messrs. Simpson of Port Adelaide announced their complete satisfaction with his term of command, their regret at his resignation at his own request, and their wish for a pleasant passage home and good fortune in whatever his new occupation should prove to be. Conrad had ended, except for brief glimpses three years later, his acquaintance with Australia and the islands of the East.

On his return to Europe in May or June 1889, he discovered that Thaddeus's worries concerning his naturalization were not unjustified. Russian procrastination is proverbial: his release from allegiance to the Tsar had indeed been notified but, besides this, Conrad had had to apply for the consent of the Governor of the Province in which he had been born, in order that he could once again enter Russian territory without difficulty. Three years had not been enough to regularize the situation. While he awaited the final document in London, he sought a new command, without success. He then began writing *Almayer's Folly* which, short though it is, occupied him intermittently for the next five years. Before leaving his first career, he had, although scarcely realizing it at the time, begun his second.

Conrad, idle in London, had indeed begun to write seriously. It was not quite a new activity—there had been the incident of *The Black Mate*. Revival arose partly, no doubt, from the immediate circumstances, first, that he had no ship, and then that he had recently completed service in a part of the world with which his imagination had been filled. By temperament a dreamer, and by gift a transmuter of dreams into concrete terms, the time had now come when he knew himself to be so overflowing with material that it must find an outlet. He had no choice but to write.

Although in point of fact it was the beginning of a new career, it was long before writing took more than a secondary place in Conrad's life. Rich and dark experience in his first calling was still to come: indeed, had he abandoned a more active life at the time that he began *Almayer's Folly*, he could never have written what is sometimes, and with reason, considered his most memorable short story, 'Heart of Darkness.' Its scene is the Congo; and how Conrad ever came to be concerned in that country is told by Marlow, the narrator in the story. 'I have a lot of relations living on the Continent,' he says. 'I am sorry to own I began to worry them. . . . I tried the women. I, Charlie Marlow, set the women to work—to get a job. Heavens!'

Such a course could only have been taken to meet a curious and perhaps a difficult ambition, related in the following words of *A Personal Record*: 'It was in 1868, when nine years old or thereabouts, that while looking at a map of Africa of the time and putting my finger on the blank space then representing the unsolved mystery of that continent, I said to myself with absolute assurance and an amazing audacity which are no longer in my character now; "When I grow up I shall go *there*!" '

It was a typical Korzeniowski whim, which his uncle Thaddeus would have understood and disapproved of. Fulfilment was carried out with Conrad's particular determination, and with consequences unhappy for himself, but fortunate for literature.

The Congo was one of the topics of the day. In 1875 Leopold II of the Belgians had founded the International Association for the Civilization of Central Africa with results as abominable for the African as they were lucrative to His Majesty. 'The vilest scramble for loot that ever disfigured the history of human conscience and geographical exploration,' Conrad later called it. Stanley's expeditions were in full flourish, and Brussels a focal point for the adventurer. Through an aunt, Conrad made application to the *Société Anonyme Belge pour le Commerce du Haut-Congo* for the command of a river steamer. Knowledge of French was of course essential, and as in this and every other way his qualifications were exceptional, a post in the company's flotilla was promised him.

He was, however, given to understand that there would be considerable delay before the appointment could be confirmed. So, placing his affairs at Brussels in the capable hands of his aunt, Mme Paradowska (to whom Marlow refers in the story quoted), Conrad deter-

mined on a brief visit to Poland to see his ailing uncle,
since Russian action had at last made this possible. They
met at Kazimierowka in the Polish Ukraine on 16
February 1890, and were together for nearly two months
—Conrad's first visit to his home and early friends for
sixteen years. He was back in Brussels by the end of
April, where the pace of events now quickened. It
appeared that one of the river-steamer captains had been
killed in a scuffle. 'It was only months and months
afterwards,' runs a passage in 'Heart of Darkness,'
'when I made an attempt to recover what was left of the
body, that I heard the original quarrel arose from a
misunderstanding about some hens. Yes, two black
hens.'

These birds were now the cause of a series of quick
interviews with 'pale plumpness in a frock coat,' of fare-
wells to his aunt, of a flying visit to London early in
May, and embarkation on the 12th in the French steamship *Ville de Maceio*, bound from Bordeaux to Teneriffe,
Dakar, Konakri, Sierra Leone, Grand Bassam, Kotonu,
Libreville, Loango, Banana at the mouth of the Congo,
and finally Boma, the seat of Government of the Free
State. Conrad would thence proceed four hundred
miles up river, to Stanley Pool.

From the point of view of his health and peace of
mind, it would have been as well had he been content
with the sight of Africa he had had from the deck
of the *Ville de Maceio*. Among his fellow-passengers was
one of the company's agents, Victor Harou, from whom
he learnt in the fullest detail the background of life in
the region for which he was setting out. 'What makes
me rather uneasy,' he wrote in a Polish letter from the
ship to his cousin Charles Zagorski, 'is the information
that sixty per cent of our company's employees return

E

to Europe before they have completed even six months'
service. Fever and dysentery! . . . Yes! But a Polish
nobleman, cased in British tar! *Nous verrons.*' It need
scarcely be said that uncle Thaddeus shared the anxieties
of the journey to the full, without any of Conrad's own
confidence and philosophy. 'In any case,' the Polish
letter continues, 'I shall console myself by remembering
—faithful to our national traditions—that it is of my
own free will that I have thrust myself into this business.'

From Boma, where he left the *Ville de Maceio*, a
smaller boat took him to Matadi, the terminal point of
navigation on the Lower Congo. 'On arriving,' says an
authority quoted by Conrad's biographer, 'one seems to
have reached an accursed land, set there as a barrier by
Nature herself, to impede all further progress.' Conrad
was over a fortnight at this place, and it seemed to him
an eternity. He then began a march of some two hundred
miles to the spot where his command was said to be
awaiting him.

Conrad made one notable acquaintance at Matadi:
this was Roger Casement, an Irishman afterwards to be
knighted, and later still to be executed for treason in the
first world war. He seemed, at the time, a fair gleam
in a sordid world. 'Thinks, speaks well, most intelligent
and very sympathetic,' Conrad noted. Thirteen years
later, in a letter to his friend Cunninghame Graham, he
says again: 'I can assure you that he is a limpid personality. There is a touch of the conquistador in him
too: for I've seen him start off into an unspeakable
wilderness swinging a crook-handled stick for all wea-
pons, with two bulldogs, Paddy (white) and Biddy
(brindle), at his heels and a Loanda boy carrying a bundle
for all company. A few months afterwards it so happened that I saw him come out again, a little leaner, a

little browner, with his stick, dogs and Loanda boy, and quietly serene as though he had been for a stroll in a park.'

Casement was an Irishman to the very core, as well as being something of a professional adventurer. The opinion may be hazarded that Conrad's acquaintance gave him an idea for the character of O'Brien in the longer of his two collaborations with Ford Madox Ford, *Romance*. There are striking resemblances between O'Brien and Casement, though it would be unwise to hunt closely for exact parallels.

Meanwhile, the march continued. It was a painful progress, and Conrad's later abhorrence of walking any distance may date from this time. Victor Harou, who was still with him, was attacked by sickness, and had to be carried for the greater part of the journey from Matadi to Manyanga, which was the immediate goal.

'Paths, paths everywhere,' to quote 'Heart of Darkness'; 'a stamped-in network of paths spreading over the empty land, through long grass, through thickets, down and up chilly ravines, up and down stony hills, ablaze with heat; and a solitude, a solitude, nobody, not a hut.' No wonder, therefore, at one of his later observations; 'a prominent characteristic of the social life here: people speaking ill of each other.'

On 8 July the party arrived at Manyanga, at which place Conrad had a bout of fever. They had sixteen days' rest. After resuming the march, Harou again fell ill, and the porters began to grumble and desert. Conrad suppressed the beginnings of a mutiny, and at last, after nine days, they arrived at Kinchassa, which was the base of the Upper Congo flotilla.

Here Conrad found that his command had been sunk in a recent accident. She had been salvaged, but would need a long repair. Unwilling to be idle and shore-bound in so wretched a place, he embarked at once as mate of the steamboat *Roi des Belges*. The master, a Dane by the name of Koch, would serve to instruct him in Congo navigation.

On 2 August the steamer, with an assistant manager and a party of agents and engineers on board, left for Stanley Falls. 'Going up that river was like travelling back to the earliest beginnings of the world, when vegetation rioted on the earth and the big trees were kings,' runs a passage in 'Heart of Darkness.' 'An empty stream, a great silence, an impenetrable forest. The air was warm, thick, heavy, sluggish. There was no joy in the brilliance of sunshine. The long stretches of the waterway ran on, deserted, into the gloom of over-shadowed distances. On silvery banks hippos and alligators sunned themselves side by side. The broadening waters flowed through a mob of wooded islands: you lost your way in that river as you would in a desert, and butted all day long against shoals, trying to find the channel, till you thought yourself bewitched and cut off for ever from everything you had known once—somewhere—far away—in another existence perhaps. There were moments when one's past came back to one, as it will sometimes when you have not a moment to spare to yourself; but it came in the shape of an unrestful and noisy dream, remembered with wonder amongst the overwhelming realities of this strange world of plants, and water, and silence. And this stillness of life did not in the least resemble a peace. It was the stillness of an implacable force brooding over an inscrutable intention. It looked at you with a vengeful aspect.'

II

In the passage quoted Conrad has summed up the very spirit of his Congo months. At the end of the journey, the purpose of which was to relieve one of the company's agents whose health was giving anxiety, they found— Kurtz. This astounding man, the central figure of 'Heart of Darkness,' with his obsession with witchcraft and the horrible practices of a dark tract of uncivilization, his uncontrollable passions, his utterly sinister personality, is unique in Conrad, and perhaps in literature. The agent, who served as the original, was named Klein, so M. Jean-Aubry tells us: a man of French nationality who died (as did Kurtz) on a river steamer.

At Stanley Falls, Captain Koch became ill: it therefore fell to Conrad to take charge of the *Roi des Belges* on her intricate passage back to the Pool. Even in his wide experience he can never have been tested more severely. It was the only fresh-water passage he ever accomplished. By the end of it he was utterly disillusioned with the job, with his employers, and the Congo. 'If you had paid any attention to my opinion in this matter,' wrote Thaddeus in a letter which reached Conrad after it was all over, 'you would have gathered I was not very enthusiastic over this plan of yours. As a Polish gentleman I have always preferred more safe and less brilliant to more brilliant and less safe.' Reading his uncle's Jeremiad, Conrad must have smiled a rueful smile.

At the end of the adventure came disagreement with the company's officials, failure to get command of a steamship to be used on a voyage of exploration, and the beginning of a serious breakdown in health. Early in November 1890 he left Kinchassa for Matadi, never to return. On the way, during the course of a river passage

in a native craft, he lost most of his belongings, except,
most happily, the incomplete manuscript of *Almayer's
Folly*. 'I arrived at that delectable capital Boma,' he says
in *A Personal Record*, 'where before the departure of the
steamer which was to take me home I had time to wish
myself dead over and over again with perfect sincerity.'

He reached Europe once more in January 1891, to face
a long illness and dreary convalescence. He never quite
shook off the effects of the Congo sickness; it is from
this time that malarial gout began to trouble him.

III

Just as Conrad was himself an artist to his finger-tips,
so there was to be a certain artistry in the shape of his
life as a sailor. He ended it, as he had begun it, in the
French service, while his last appointment of consequence
was in the *Torrens*, one of the most beautiful sailing ships
ever built. She was called the Wonderful *Torrens*; and
she was, in Conrad's own words, 'one of the fastest and
for many years the favourite passenger ship to Adelaide.'

Before that appointment, there had been a tedious
period in the German hospital in London, followed, in
May 1891, by a visit to a hydropathic establishment at
Champel near Geneva. While there, he finished the
eighth chapter of *Almayer's Folly*, and there he was offered
the chance of return to Africa, to command a ship
navigating the Niger. He refused. For a time, immediately following his recovery, he accepted employment
as manager of a Thames waterside warehouse. Then
came the posting as chief officer in the *Torrens*, and a
return to that deep-water seamanship in which, for all its
ardours and endurances, he saw the opportunity for
peace of mind and a restoration of health in body.

Fine ship as the *Torrens* was, her luck appeared to have changed with her masters. Captain Angel had built up her reputation, but on her first voyage under Captain Cope she had lost her foremast in a squall, and part of her cargo had been burnt. On her second, she seemed to have forgotten her capacity for speed. Conrad, who signed on in November 1891, made the passage to Adelaide in ninety-five days: not a fast one, but pleasant. She left for London on 7 April, touching at Capetown and St. Helena, being home again in the late summer.

The round voyage, now so familiar to Conrad, did him all the good he had expected. Wisely, therefore, he continued, leaving London on 25 October 1892 and making Adelaide ninety-seven days later. It was on this voyage out that, for the first time in his life, he discussed with another being the literary project he had now been nursing for so long.

Among the passengers in the *Torrens* was a young Cambridge man, by name W. H. Jacques. He was a great reader, and he and Conrad had many wide-ranging discussions. One day, an opening was made which probably demanded a good deal of courage from Conrad. 'Would it bore you very much reading an MS. in a hand-writing like mine?' he asked Jacques. 'Not at all,' said Jacques. 'Next day . . . Jacques entered my cabin,' says Conrad in *A Personal Record*. 'He had a thick, woollen muffler round his throat and the MS. was in his hand. He tendered it to me with a steady look, but without a nod. I took it in silence. He sat down on the couch and still said nothing. I opened and shut a drawer under my desk, on which a filled-up log-slate lay wide open in its wooden frame, waiting to be copied neatly into the sort of book I was accustomed to write with care, the ship's log-book. I turned my back squarely on the desk. And even then

Jacques never offered a word. "Well, what do you say?"
I asked at last. "Is it worth finishing?" This question
expressed exactly the whole of my thoughts.

' "Distinctly," he answered in his sedate, veiled voice,
and then coughed a little.

' "Were you interested?" I inquired further, almost in
a whisper.

' "Very much! . . ."

' "Now let me ask you one more thing: is the story
quite clear to you as it stands?"

'He raised his dark, gentle eyes to my face and seemed
surprised.

' "Yes! Perfectly."

'This was all I was to hear from his lips concerning
the merits of *Almayer's Folly*. We never spoke together
of the book again.'

The incident occurred just as the *Torrens* was about to
double the Cape. Jacques died shortly after reaching
Australia.

IV

'It is certain,' said a sage, 'my conviction gains
infinitely the moment another soul will believe in it.'
Conrad was fond of quoting this sentence, and every
artist will know why. Melancholy Jacques; he had
witnessed a crisis, in which his own part was an odd one.
Had he been enthusiastic, Conrad would have been
pleased and stimulated. Conrad's contacts with well-
educated English people were then rare, and he had discovered that Jacques was a man of discrimination. Had
he been indifferent, or rather perhaps, a touch more
indifferent, Conrad would without question have been
discouraged and might even have destroyed his story. As
it was, the lack of any strongly expressed opinion had

the effect of deferring work on the novel. Conrad's feeling about it seems to have become suspended. Then came an ironic circumstance, which he would at a later time have appreciated. Another young man took passage in the *Torrens*, equally cultivated, equally friendly, and much more forthcoming. His name was John Galsworthy. Conrad and he got on famously. It was the beginning of a life-long friendship: but Conrad did not again take out *Almayer* from its drawer, although Galsworthy's opinion even as a youth would have been of value.

To many people of literary bent come such incidents as that in which Jacques was concerned. Not many are shown the first sustained work of a great writer, and not many make exactly the right remarks. It must always be to Jacques's credit that his laconic answers were at least on the right lines. Stimulating critics are as rare, perhaps, as good writers. It was Conrad's future fortune to have knowledge of both.

Meanwhile, the *Torrens* had rounded the Cape, made Adelaide, and returned home. She had carried Galsworthy from Adelaide as far as the Cape, and a schoolmaster, E. L. Sanderson, who was also to become one of Conrad's closest friends. He and Galsworthy had set out to see R. L. Stevenson, and had failed. They sailed home with the future author of *Nostromo*, and found the experience rewarding.

Galsworthy recorded later that, when he joined the ship in Adelaide harbour in March 1893, Conrad was fighting a fire in the hold. 'None of us passengers knew it till long after,' he said. His portrait of Conrad is one of the best we have. 'Very dark he looked in the burning sunlight, tanned, with a peaked brown beard, almost black hair, and dark brown eyes, over which the lids were deeply folded. He was thin, not tall, his arms very long, his shoulders broad, his head set rather forward. He spoke to me with a strong foreign accent. . . . A good seaman, watchful of the weather; quick in handling the ship: considerate with the apprentices—we had a lonely, unhappy Belgian youth among them, who took unhandily to the sea and dreaded going aloft. Conrad compassionately spared him all he could. With the crew he was popular: they were individuals to him, not a mere gang . . . with the young second mate, a cheerful capable young seaman, very English, he was friendly; and respectful, if faintly ironic, with his whiskered, stout old captain. Evening watches in fine weather we spent on the poop. Ever the great teller of a tale, he had already nearly twenty years of tales to tell. Tales of ships and storms, of Polish revolution, of his youthful Carlist gun-running adventure, of the Malay seas, and the Congo . . . and I remember feeling that he outweighed for me all the other experiences of that voyage. Fascination was Conrad's great characteristic—the fascination of vivid expressiveness and zest, of his deeply affectionate heart, and his far-ranging, subtle mind.'

V

The *Torrens* reached London, after another slow passage, on 26 July 1893. Conrad found a letter from his uncle urging him to revisit Poland. He did so, spending August and September at Kazimierowka, and seeing his Zagorski cousins at Lublin.

Captain Cope, worried at the failure of the *Torrens* to live up to her clipper fame for speed, was taking steps to transfer to steam, and there seemed a chance that Conrad might succeed him. It was one he would have welcomed, but in the end it was not vouchsafed him.

In *Last Essays* he wrote: 'I ceased to "belong to her" as the saying is (it was a wrench) on the 15th of October 1893, when, in London Dock, I took a long look from the quay at that last of ships I ever had under my care, and, stepping round the corner of a tall warehouse, parted from her for ever, and at the same time stepped (in merciful ignorance) out of my sea life altogether.'

It was nearly true, but not quite, for at the end of the same year he took a French steamer, the *Adowa*, across the Channel. She was intended to carry Canadian emigrants from Rouen. She reached Rouen on 4 December, sailing into a frozen scene such as Conrad had known at Amsterdam years before. Great lumps of ice were floating down the Seine; and not an emigrant appeared. Thirty days later, Conrad received orders to take the ship back to London. She arrived on 12 January 1894, when her acting master gave up what was in truth his last command.

As a career, that of the sea was now ended for Conrad, but there were to be later episodes not without their pleasure. He took to sailing the Kent and Essex waters in the company of friends; he was at sea, at the request of the Admiralty, with a special service vessel for a short spell in the first world war; and he crossed and re-crossed the Atlantic at the close of his life under conditions very different from anything he had known hitherto.

His professional seafaring may well end with a tribute he received in the last year of his life from one who had served as an apprentice under his charge. 'I gather that you have a son,' said the writer: 'if this is so, may I say something in this letter to him? I dislike flattery in any form, but I would like him to realize what a marvellous personality you have. I have loved you more than any man I ever knew except my own father. . . .'

ASHORE

I

THE old life was over, the new not yet begun. And as if to mark the pause, on 29 January 1894 there came news of the death of his uncle Thaddeus at Kazimierowka. He left Conrad a small sum of twelve hundred roubles. He had been, in the words of *A Personal Record*, 'for a quarter of a century the wisest, the firmest, the most indulgent of guardians, extending over me a paternal care and affection, a moral support which I seemed to feel always near me in the most distant parts of the earth.'

They had met only four times in twenty years, but the reunions had been of reasonable length, long enough for Conrad to feel that Poland had ties and charm. For a while, ashore, and feeling the sense of isolation—which was never far from him—stronger than ever, he was driven in upon himself, and his first sustained effort was to complete *Almayer's Folly*. It was finally corrected, and made ready for another eye than that of Jacques, on 22 May 1894. He sent it to a publisher, by messenger, from the offices of the Shipmasters Society—his choice falling upon T. Fisher Unwin, a patron of letters, then and later, of considerable reputation. 'Acceptance,' said Conrad in a letter twenty-four years afterwards, 'came some three months later, in the first typewritten letter I ever received in my life.' He could scarcely have realized his own good fortune, so contrary to general experience—that a first work of originality and merit should have found a place in the list of the first firm to which it was sent. The event was not unique; but it was uncommon.

Quite inexperienced as he was in the ways (as opposed to the products) of writers, Conrad could not then know, and does not appear later to have realized, what an unusual case his was. Of his intellectual and emotional equipment something has already been said: it was remarkable enough. So was the rich material with which life had already presented him. Seldom would he have to meet a writer's common problem—lack of a plot.

He was, in the later thirties, a man of a maturity to which many never attain. The urge to write came from within, and was insistent. Best of all, his mental as opposed to his bodily energy was liberal and untapped. Never had he need to assume an attitude, for his was already moulded. Had he been more familiar with the world of letters, less deeply pessimistic, he would have recognized a miracle, of which he was the subject.

Miracles need agents for their fulfilment. Again he was blessed; for in his case it was Edward Garnett, a man younger than himself, a professional reader who was then advising Fisher Unwin. Garnett was one who, in the course of a life devoted to the discovery of talent, founded the reputation of more than one publishing firm which still flourishes. Some men can sustain this life of often ill-rewarded search, and achieve creative work of their own. More often they become merely the midwives of letters. Few emerge from the grind as well as Garnett did. There is a scene in that otherwise imperfect collaboration between Conrad and Ford Madox Ford, *The Inheritors*, in which such a servant of letters is described at work. Usually they are spared close scrutiny, just as they are spared meeting with authors whose work they reject, but occasionally they seek acquaintance with their 'discoveries.' It was so now.

Garnett, who by one of those minor wonders of human capacity kept his taste inviolate throughout his life, immediately understood the rare quality of Conrad's work. It is easy enough now to see why. It was particularly creditable in the early nineties.

Shortly after the acceptance of *Almayer's Folly*, Fisher Unwin arranged the meeting between author and reader. They found an instant sympathy, which turned into a permanent friendship. Garnett gave Conrad the encouragement he needed; his praise was discriminating, his knowledge of the world of letters considerable. His father was the celebrated Dr. Richard Garnett, a high official in the British Museum, and the author of *The Twilight of the Gods*; his wife was the skilled translator of Tchekov and other Russian writers; his son became the author of *Lady into Fox*. The Garnetts were, and are, of the aristocracy of letters. Nearly thirty years later Conrad wrote to Garnett: 'The generosity of your criticism, my dear Edward, is great enough to put heart into a dead man. . . . The belief in the absolute unflawed honesty of your judgment has been one of the mainstays of my literary life. . . . In all your literary judgments there is never anything suspect. Your very prejudices are genuinely personal and, in a manner of speaking, can be thoroughly trusted. . . . It is good to write while there is a reader like you about.'

The contract for *Almayer* had been settled by August 1894. The book appeared on 29 April of the year following. Meanwhile Conrad was enjoying some leisure, the result of his uncle's legacy, and had been sailing an eighteen-ton cutter with his friend Mr. G. F. W. Hope.

Some proofs were, in fact, corrected on board. And in November 1894, even before the appearance of *Almayer*, he had begun another novel, *An Outcast of the Islands*. The background was the same, but in sequence of event it should actually have come before *Almayer*.

Conrad had not yet come to the final decision to make writing his profession. In a note which he wrote for later editions of the *Outcast* he said: 'Neither in my mind nor in my heart had I then given up the sea. . . . A phrase of Edward Garnett's is, as a matter of fact, responsible for this book. One evening, when we had dined together and he had listened to an account of my perplexities (I fear he must have been growing a little tired of them) he pointed out that there was no need to determine my future absolutely. Then he added: "You have the style, you have the temperament; why not write another?" Had he said, "Why not go on writing?" it is very probable that he would have scared me away from pen and ink for ever; but there was nothing either to frighten one or to arouse one's antagonism in the mere suggestion to "write another." '

If Conrad is to be believed, it was this fortunate turn of a remark which decided his future. In fact, it is unlikely that anything that anyone had then said would have deterred him from his new line of exploration. Words mattered to Conrad and, although many a writer is said to have been frozen by a phrase or a sentence of condemnation, it is questionable if this has ever happened when compulsion was upon them. Conrad had already received the first great stimulus of acceptance, and was, in actual fact, fairly launched into his new career.

II

Conrad's second novel, took considerably less time to write than *Almayer*, not because he had set himself an easier task but because he had less distraction. It occupied him during the winter of 1894 and for most of the following year. He tried London, Brussels, finally Champel in Switzerland as places in which to work. Champel was best: it had proved so with *Almayer* and it did so now. Many years later, when he came to write *Under Western Eyes*, Conrad had some rather sharp things to say of the atmosphere of Switzerland, but there is no question that it was congenial to his moods as a writer.

By September, the *Outcast* was finished and publication had been arranged, again with Fisher Unwin. From now onwards, in his biographer's words, 'the main adventures of Conrad's life are those connected with his books.' The change from the life of a professional wanderer was not altogether for the better. Never an easy writer, though always a determined and a conscientious one, Conrad had now put his hand to the task of earning his bread solely by work of a highly serious kind. It was fortunate that he did not know the world of letters from within, as did his friend Garnett, who could have told him (had he been foolish enough to do so), of the immense difficulties likely to be met with by a writer with nothing of the hack in his composition. Such rare people should always be endowed with private means.

Added to the obstacles which lay ahead, after his return from the Congo Conrad's health was never again well established. Gout, of the old-fashioned kind which makes for a peppery temper, was his most serious and recurrent affliction; and indeed, admirable as his letters

Joseph Conrad
in 1924

The ' Wonderful ' Torrens

are, his constant preoccupation with his ailments is the one respect in which, over the years, they are apt to become tedious. Sympathy is not always a constant sentiment, and a tale of woes, protracted from year to year, is apt to cloy. Conrad suffered, there is no question, and a background of physical discomfort, often amounting to actual pain, must always be recollected in considering his output.

An Outcast appeared in March 1896. It was delayed by a fire at the printers, though by more recent standards the speed of its publication may seem exceptional. Almost simultaneously, he took another step which, whatever the omens may then have appeared to be, proved one of the wisest of his life. He married Miss Jessie George, a young girl whose acquaintance he had made some eighteen months earlier at the house of his friends, the Hopes.

Miss George was the daughter of a bookseller. She herself wrote in a modest way, and indeed two years after Conrad's death she published a book of reminiscences, *Joseph Conrad as I knew him*, which, although without literary pretensions, related in a graphic way many of the difficulties in marriage to a highly strung, artistic foreigner, apt to succumb to strange illnesses, and one whom the sea had made incurably restless. Jessie Conrad was attractive, maternal and quite undeterred by practical difficulties. Conrad's friends were glad of the match; the pair, with the two boys, Borys and John, born to them later, were to make a most united family.

In later years, as the result of a very bad fall, Mrs. Conrad's own health was as precarious as that of her husband; but her care, common sense and loyalty never failed him. She took a helpful interest in his writing,

F

often acting as his secretary, and indeed made one further strong and lasting reason for his admiration of the English. No marriage of a man of letters could have been better contrived, and the trials which Mrs. Conrad herself relates were chiefly those of circumstance. It was years before they could feel any real sense of security.

On 24 March 1896 the newly wedded pair embarked at Southampton for St. Malo. They spent the first few months of their married life at a house in the Ile-Grande, near Lannion. Conrad's own description of the scenery, which appears in a letter of 14 April to E. L. Sanderson, is a good example of one aspect of his style. 'The coast is rocky, sandy, wild and full of mournful expressiveness,' he says. 'But the land, at the back of the wide stretches of the sea enclosed by the barren archipelago, is green and smiling and sunny—often even when the sea and the islets are under the shadow of the passing clouds. From beyond the rounded slopes of the hill the sharp spires of many village churches point persistently to the sky. And the people that inhabits these shores is a people of women—a black-clad and white-capped—for the men fish in Iceland or on the banks of Newfoundland. Only here and there a rare old fellow with long hair, forgotten by the successive roll-calls of the sea, creeps along the rock between beaches and looks sad and useless and lone in the stony landscape.'

In Brittany he wrote one story, 'The Idiots,' published later in *Tales of Unrest*—the only instance of his immediate use of material lying at hand. He also began *The Rescue*, a further Malayan tale. 'If the virtues of Lingard please most of the critics,' he wrote to his publisher, 'they shall have more of them.' They did: but not then. *The Rescue* was in fact put aside, and only completed after more than twenty years. With *Almayer* and *An Outcast* it concludes what may be called the Lingard cycle, though the novels are written in the reverse of chronological order.

In the autumn of 1896 the Conrads returned to England, at first settling in the village of Stanford-le-Hope, Essex, near some friends. Here Conrad, setting aside *The Rescue*, began *The Nigger of the 'Narcissus'*, which, he told Garnett, was to enshrine his former shipmates 'in a decent edifice.' It is a story of bad weather, defeated by the determination of a ship's company; just as in the later companion-piece, *Typhoon*, the storm is defeated by the skill of a ship's captain. It is noteworthy that the original title of *The Nigger* was *The Forecastle: A Tale of Ship and Men*. This is accurate description. The ship, not the nigger, is the true theme of the book: and in it, perhaps for the clearest time, are to be heard the precise accents of nineteenth-century forecastle hands.

The difficulties which Conrad had in order to secure a living from his writing are often emphasized. As against this, two facts should be noted. He seldom had trouble, from the first, in finding a market for his wares, even if this appeared to him an unsatisfactory one. Not only book publishers, but editors of reputable magazines both in England and America were generally glad to buy his work. Conrad thought in large terms: a more realistic experience would have shown him that, for a writer of his calibre, he had little of which to complain. Moreover, he was from the first appreciated by men whose opinion counted. First there was Garnett. Then, in May 1896, H. G. Wells wrote a most discerning and appreciative notice of *An Outcast* in *The Saturday Review*. He called it 'the finest piece of fiction that has been published this year. . . . Surely this is real

romance, the romance that is real. He imagines his
scenes and their sequence like a master, he knows his
individualities to their hearts.'

Others followed: Cunninghame Graham, W. H.
Hudson, Henley, E. V. Lucas, Galsworthy, Henry James,
Edward Thomas, Bennett, Kipling, Stephen Crane,
Edmund Gosse. There was scarcely a writer of importance who did not soon appreciate Conrad's work at its
proper value. If the public were behindhand in their
admiration, they followed at last. Conrad had, in fact,
no case for just complaint at neglect, either in this
country, America, or elsewhere, for his work was translated (though somewhat spasmodically) from his earliest
days as a novelist.

Diverse in personality and in literary calibre as these
friends of Conrad's were, they had one characteristic in
common. Not merely did they live by, and deeply care
for, letters; they were craftsmen interested in writing
as a fine and difficult art. They perceived in Conrad not
a rival—he was always too unlike anyone but himself to
create direct professional jealousy—but a man who was
doing things differently, with increasing skill, and with
his whole mind and heart. They understood his 'shop,'
as he did theirs, slowly at first, but soon completely.

Cunninghame Graham, together with Galsworthy and
Stephen Crane, had the closest personal friendships with
him: Conrad admired their works, as they came from
the press, and expressed his feeling in letters overflowing with appreciation, though it is certain he
realized that Henry James was, in a technical sense, a
better writer than anyone else of his acquaintance. The
pains which James bestowed upon his work, his intense
devotion to his calling, were commensurate with
Conrad's own incessant toil and single-mindedness.

They were never very close in method, but each could measure justly the full worth of the other. James's balanced praise probably meant more to the inmost Conrad than that of any other writer.

On the business side of his affairs, Conrad depended greatly upon J. B. Pinker, who was then engaged in what was the novel trade of literary agent. He left much in Pinker's hands; his trust in him was steadfast. Although it was long before he was free from material cares, at least he did not need to do his own bargaining with editors and publishers. He was able to concentrate upon his family and his writing. Ford Madox Ford has recorded that for years Conrad had what amounted almost to an obsession that his family were in danger of starving. This was because he had at heart no illusions as to the quality of his own work, and realized almost from the first that his success would depend not upon pot-boilers, which men such as Bennett and Lucas could pour forth apparently at will, but upon the loyalty of an intelligent and informed public, one which could never be numbered in millions. And yet, paradoxically, he seems never, in these earlier writing years, to have abandoned the unreasonable hope that, without lowering his standards one shade, he could yet reach what was called the 'great heart of the public.' He felt that in this, as in so many other ways, he might prove to be an exception; literary history proved them not unknown. In later years, indeed, events did something to justify his faith.

*   *   *

Conrad himself set great store by *The Nigger of the 'Narcissus'*, and its lack of instant success disappointed him. It was published in book form in December 1897. In the following month his first child, Borys, was born. In

March, *Tales of Unrest*, his first book of stories, appeared on the market. This included 'Karain, a Memory'; 'The Idiots'; 'An Outpost of Progress'; 'The Return' and 'The Lagoon.' Of the five tales 'An Outpost of Progress,' Conrad's lesser fragment from the Congo, was by far the most important. It does not equal 'Heart of Darkness,' but it foreshadows it.

After a further try at continuing *The Rescue* he wrote that notable autobiographical story 'Youth' in the course of a few days. He did this for *Blackwood's Magazine*, with which he long had particular sympathy. He wrote a year or so later to Sir Algernon Methuen: 'Apart from my friendly relations, *Blackwood* is the only periodical always open to me—and is the only one for which I really care to write.'

Mood and outlook fitted. *Blackwood* had, and has, a tradition of action, clarity and colourful background. It has always been read by men of catholic tastes, with certain conservative standards of conduct thoroughly understood by Conrad. There is, indeed, a sort of composite 'Maga' man—and he is Marlow, Conrad's narrator: a man supposedly of few words in normal times, but capable, when stimulated by the right company, of detailed, salty narrative. It was not often perhaps that Conrad was aware of addressing a particular public, but when *Blackwood* was in question, he could assume its mantle not only with ease but relish. There are those who find Marlow a bore: but he had his purpose. He removed Conrad one degree from his story, which was sometimes useful, while he and his friends were very obviously members of the *Blackwood* fraternity. It may be argued, in fact, that in this particular instance, and this alone, his known audience had a definite effect upon his prose style. Mr. Blackwood, editor of 'Maga,' obviously approved of Marlow and his brand of talk. No wonder, therefore, that Conrad became an established contributor.

As *The Rescue* once more proved intractable, Conrad, recognizing temporary defeat, began a novel with a new setting, *Lord Jim*. Although not equal to his very best, it is the book by which he is most widely known. Yet during the time of its actual writing, he was sufficiently depressed about his financial prospects to have journeyed to Glasgow in the hopes of receiving a sea command through the influence of Cunninghame Graham. 'Nothing decisive happened,' he records. 'My impression is that a command will come out of it sooner or later—most likely later, when the pressing need is past and I have found my way on shore.'

Meanwhile, he moved from Essex to Pent Farm, near Hythe in Kent. Here he flourished, not financially, but in the quality and substance of his output. 'Youth' was followed by 'Heart of Darkness,' which is possibly the finest of all his stories. At the beginning of 1899 he obtained a prize of fifty guineas from the *Academy*, for his *Tales of Unrest*; and in the year following, *Lord Jim* began to be serialized in 'Maga,' actually before it was completed. In March he wrote to Garnet: 'I am old and sick and in debt—but lately I have found I can still write. *It* comes, *it* comes and I am young and healthy and rich.'

He finished *Lord Jim* in July 1900, and then went with his family to Bruges, to join Ford Madox Ford (then called Hueffer), with whom he had already begun to collaborate. During the winter of 1900 and the earlier part of 1901 he wrote 'Typhoon;' 'Falk'—a story of his first command—'Amy Foster;' a study of a shipwrecked foreigner's sad adventures in this country; and he set to work on *Romance*, the second, the longer and by far the more important of his two ventures with Ford.

The first, *The Inheritors—an Extravagant Story*, had been published with little success in 1901. It was a satire on contemporary Europe, and did not succeed artistically or in any other way. 'The main idea was wholly F.M.H.,' he told Mr. Curle later, 'as also most of the details.' But *Romance*, an adventure story of the West Indies, was worthy of his metal. It is gripping stuff from first to last, and it had a limited but thoroughly deserved success.

Conrad wrote the following note in T. J. Wise's copy of a later edition: 'The tale as it stands here is based on Ford Madox Hueffer's MS. of *Seraphina*, a much shorter work and quite different in tone. On this we went to work together, developing the action and adding some new characters. We collaborated right through, but it may be said that the middle part of the book is mainly mine with bits of F.M.H. while the first part is wholly out of *Seraphina*: the second part is almost wholly so. The last part is certainly three-quarters MS. F.M.H., with here and there a par by me.'

It may be said that *Romance* is creditable to both parties. It is a story which has lost nothing of excitement and atmosphere in the course of time: an historical novel showing, among other things, the bloodiness of Caribbean pirates as known to their law-abiding contemporaries: and the deep clash of Protestant and Catholic, both in creed and outlook, in distant quarters of the earth.

The year 1902 was spent in completing *Romance*, and in writing that remarkable story, 'The End of the Tether.' Then, from the beginning of 1903 to September 1904,

Conrad engaged himself on the most ambitious task of his whole literary life. He wrote *Nostromo*, and so created a Central American republic.

Never a dabbler, but a man to whom serious work of any kind entailed complete absorption, Conrad has recalled his own state when writing *Nostromo*, in a passage in *A Personal Record*. 'For twenty months,' he says, 'neglecting the common joys of life that fall to the lot of the humblest on this earth, I had, like the prophet of old, "wrestled with the Lord" for my creation, for the headlands of the coast, for the darkness of the Placid Gulf, the light on the snows, the clouds on the sky, and for the breath of life that had to be blown into the shapes of men and women, of Latin and Saxon, of Jew and Gentile. These are, perhaps, strong words, but it is difficult to characterize otherwise the intimacy and the strain of a creative effort in which mind and will and conscience are engaged to the full hour after hour, day after day, away from the world, and to the exclusion of all that makes life really lovable and gentle—something for which a material parallel can only be found in the everlasting sombre stress of the westward winter passage round Cape Horn. For that too is the wrestling of men with the might of their Creator, in a great isolation from the world, without the amenities and consolations of life, a lonely struggle under a sense of overmatched littleness, for no reward that could be adequate, but for the mere winning of a longitude.'

Such was his concentration. His few distractions were equally individual. He would from time to time break away to write a few pages of *The Mirror of the Sea*, a transition from a wide canvas to a smaller one—some would say, from a major classic to a smaller but more delightful one. Ill health continually unnerved him; so did financial worries, including the failure of a bank which had advanced him money.

Nothing in his career disappointed him quite so much as the failure of *Nostromo* to secure immediately that wider public he would so much have enjoyed, and for which he continued to hope. Such great effort had gone into its composition, that it seemed impossible it could meet the same fate as its predecessors—discriminating appreciation, followed by no large popular audience. Yet this was so. *Nostromo* is unquestionably a great book: Dr. F. R. Leavis rightly refers to its Elizabethan quality. It is certainly a noble feat of the imagination. Nevertheless it is the diversion, the companion-piece, the very personal *The Mirror of the Sea* which has always called forth more general affection.

III

Conrad, in a letter to Mr. Richard Curle, once expressed a hope that, in writing about his work, Mr. Curle might help to 'save my hide from being permanently tarred.' In another letter to an American, he said: 'My only sea-book, and the only tribute to a life which I have lived in my own particular way, is *The Mirror of the Sea*.' Although this sentence contains exaggeration, it is true enough that *The Mirror of the Sea* is a maritime record of a very special kind. Had he written nothing else, it would have gained its particular niche among those books, written by seamen for seamen, of which another notable example is *The Brassbounder*, written from comparable experience by his friend, Sir David Bone.

The qualities which make *The Mirror* unique are its beauty of language and its blend of remembrance, appraisal, and historical sidelight. It has outline rather than form. Pressed by a publisher for a 'blurb' with which to usher it before the public (a task which needs a touch which few possess, and for which many feel distaste), he wrote: 'The book is an imaginative rendering of a reminiscent mood. . . . It is also a record of a phase, now nearly vanished, of a certain kind of activity, sympathetic to the inhabitants of this island. It is likewise an attempt to set down graphically certain genuine feelings and emotions born from the experience of a respectable and useful calling, which, at the same time, happens to be of national importance. It may be defined as a discourse (with a personal note) on ships, seamen and the sea.'

The theme is sail and the sailor. Conrad disregarded steam, since in his opinion the steamship demanded little art in management, and no love. Sail and its technique demanded everything of a man: his skill, his judgment, strength, faith in their entirety. Conrad was acutely aware that he had, in his professional life, lived through the final years of a creation of man's hands which was steeped in beauty, and which had an immense history. The sailing ship, it was evident to him, had demanded the same skill from the time of Ulysses and long before him, to that of the gracious clippers in which he had himself served. He felt the irony of the fact that the coming of steam had stimulated the builder of sailing ships to his greatest triumphs, to the highest grace; and at that very point his honoured craft had at last become an anachronism, or at best one to be exercised henceforth on craft built only for pleasure.

We witness to-day almost the same fate overtaking steam. Conrad wrote: 'whatever craft he handles with skill, the seaman of the future shall be not our descendant, but only our successor . . . History repeats itself, but the special call of an art which has passed away is never reproduced.' He summed up a matter which had more than the particular application he intended.

Another quality which made Conrad's book singular was the fact that his unusual sea apprenticeship had freed him from the antagonisms and jealousies which sometimes create a barrier between the merchant sea-men and those whose duty lies with the King's ships. Hence his tributes, which have never been excelled, and only equalled by the American historian Mahan, to Nelson and the navy of his time, which was that of the golden age of sail's supremacy. 'Exalt! the word seems to be created for the man,' he wrote. 'Not the least glory of the Navy is that it understood Nelson. . . . He brought heroism into the line of duty. Verily he is a terrible ancestor.' 'The God of gales and battles, favouring her arms to the last, has let the sun of England's sailing fleet and of its greatest master set in unclouded glory. . . .' As he pointed out, in words which again derived from direct experience, the greatness of Nelson and his band of brothers was enhanced by the quality of his foes, as represented by the navies of France and Spain.

Fragments of the philosophy and vision which inform *The Mirror* are to be found in some of his letters. 'The naval training,' he wrote to his friend Mrs. Sanderson in 1917, 'has a peculiar quality, and forms a very fine type. For one thing, it is strictly methodized to a very definite end, which is noble in itself and of a very high idealistic nature, while on its technical side it deals with a body of systemized facts which cannot be discussed apart from their reality,—say, on the ground of personal taste, for instance. That steadies the young intelligence and faces it with life, not as it is written about but as it actually is.'

At the time he wrote, he was recently back from a spell at sea with a flotilla on service in the first world war. 'Last year,' he continued, 'I saw many naval officers from Admirals to Sub-Lieutenants, and I have noticed that the Navy thinks rightly on all questions. I don't say this in the sense of the Navy thinking as I do. But whatever conclusion a naval officer arrives at, even if distasteful to me, I can't help recognizing that he arrives at it on sound grounds, making use of his intelligence. . . . Coming on shore I went into a couple of drawing-rooms and one or two newspaper offices; and what I heard there made painful contrast.' Due allowance must be made for the immediate impact of war, but Conrad's view did not then differ fundamentally from what he had long felt.

Again, in a letter to the ship-owner Laurence Holt, he said: 'A year, or a year and a half of training in a seagoing sailing ship I would regard for a boy destined for the sea as a course in classical practice of the sea. What he will actually learn on board that ship he will leave behind him directly he steps on the deck of a modern steamship. But he will have acquired the old lore of the sea, which has fashioned so many generations down to his very fathers, and in its essence will remain with the future generations of seamen, even after the day when the last sail and the last oar have vanished from the waters of our globe.'

His last sea-voyage of any length merely confirmed all that he had written and felt many years before. 'In the early part of last year,' he wrote in 1924 to a fellow-seaman, 'I crossed to New York with my old friend

Captain David Bone, commanding the *Tuscania*. Of course I was made free of the bridge and the navigation room. I won't say I was not interested. I was, in a way, for about thirty hours, till I went twice over all the switches working various gadgets. But I remained cold, completely cold, before all those things which make the position of a ship's officer almost an indoor occupation. It is a fact that one can take a ship along now in white gloves and without, so to speak, opening one's mouth once. There were seven officers there and they were very charming to the old veteran; it was rather a special crowd since only two of them, juniors, had never set foot on the deck of a sailing vessel. Captain Bone, who had some ten years of sail, told me that they had wholly lost the "weather sense," that touch with the natural phenomena of wind and sea which was the very breath of our professional life.'

Captain Bone himself recorded the passing of the older generation in *The Brassbounder*. His affectionate farewell to the *City of Florence*, barque of Glasgow, is almost another reflection from *The Mirror*. Of the men who manned and steered her, he said truly that they were 'scattered afar on seven seas, learning a new way of seafaring; turning the grip that had held to a life aloft to the heft of a coalman's shovel, the deft fingers that had fashioned a wondrous plan of stay and shroud to the touch of winch, valve and lever.'

It is as well to make clear that although Conrad was classical in his attitude to the sea and seamanship, he was never hidebound. Very early in his life he had accepted service in steam. He knew the life well, and although he regretted the passing of a great art, that of the management and navigation of the full-rigged ship, he realized that her practical utility, except for purposes of training, had gone for ever. Moreover, when he could find stimulus and refreshment in new inventions, he seized opportunity eagerly. At an age when many would have hesitated, in view of the flimsy structures used by the airmen of the earlier years of the first world war, he was taken, at his own request, on a flight patrol with a naval pilot. He enjoyed every second of his hour and twenty minutes in a Short biplane. 'I reckon it like a miser counting his hoard,' he said afterwards, noticing 'the sense of security, so much more perfect than in any small boat I've ever been in,' and flight's mysterious fascination, 'whose invisible wing had touched my heart up there.'

It reflects the spirit of a man who had retained elasticity. He was, at the time, nearly sixty and racked with gout.

IV

With *Nostromo* at last finished, *The Mirror* in train, and his wife suffering in her knee from the effects of a fall which she was to feel for the rest of her life, Conrad took his small family to Capri in the hope that (like their young friend Norman Douglas) he would find the climate and place inspiring. It did not prove so. Even the weather failed him and, as his health continued indifferent, the Conrads left by sea for Marseilles. It was the first time he had returned there for nearly twenty years; but, although he enjoyed his visit, he could make no progress with a large-scale Mediterranean novel, on which his heart was now set.

He was summoned home to see a stage version of 'To-morrow' (one of the stories in the *Typhoon* volume) performed by the Stage Society. It was well received, and this gratified Conrad, though it brought no financial benefit. In the years of his fame, a dramatized version of *The Secret Agent*, one of his most important novels, was staged in London, though again without commercial good fortune.

In the later part of the year 1905 he continued writing *The Mirror of the Sea*, and completed a story, 'The Informer,' which was to appear in the collection called *A Set of Six*. In 1906 he again spent some months in France, this time at Montpelier, where he revised *The Mirror* and wrote a great part of *The Secret Agent*. This time the stay was an entire success. The climate of Languedoc did him good, and he enjoyed the French atmosphere with which he was so familiar. In the summer he returned to London, staying in the house of John Galsworthy in Addison Road, where he was particularly well looked after, and where he wrote, to the accompaniment of innumerable cigarettes, in a little house at the end of the garden. In London, on 2 August, his second son John was born.

In October *The Mirror* appeared. It was received with gratifying warmth, and drew forth many expressions of praise, including one from Kipling, whose enthusiasm particularly pleased Conrad. In November appeared *The Secret Agent*. No writer has ever produced, concurrently, more different books. *The Mirror* has been described already. *The Secret Agent* is a study of the London international underworld. It called forth unstinted praise from, among others, Arnold Bennett, who said that while it was the kind of thing 'I reckon to handle myself, I respectfully retire from the comparison.'

In December, Conrad returned to Montpelier, which had so charmed him earlier in the year. There he toyed once more with the idea of his Mediterranean novel, and completed 'The Duel,' a short story with a background

Don Pépé Hill *calm* stroked his grey and pendent moustache, whose long fine ends hung below the clean cut line of his jaw, and spoke with conscious pride in his reputation.

"So padre I don't know what will happen. This I know that Don Carlos can speak to that macaque Pedrito Montero and threaten the destruction of the mine with perfect assurance that he will be taken seriously. For people know me."

He began to turn the cigar in lips a little nervously and went on

"But that is talk — work for the politicos. I am a military man. I do not know what may happen but I know what ought to be done. The mine should march upon the town with guns, axes, knives tied up to sticks, por Dios. Only.... on hill."

His hands twitched. The cigar turned faster in the the corner of the lips.

"And who should lead but I? Unfortunately, observe, I have given my word not to let the mine fall into the hands of these thieves, and in war — you know, mi padre — the fate of battles is uncertain — and whom could I leave here. The explosives are ready. But it would require a man of honour, of intelligence, of judgment, of courage. Another old officer of Paez — or — or — perhaps one of Paez old chaplains..."

He got up long, lank, upright hard with his martial moustache and the bony structure of his face from which the sunken eyes seemed to pierce the priest who stood still an empty snuff box held upside down in his hand and glared back at the governor of the mine.

→ to recto

A page of manuscript from Nostromo

Joseph Conrad
Sept. 1923

LOW

of French military life, and with an atmosphere, for once, of comedy. He also began work on *Chance*, a novel which, like *The Rescue*, proved intractable.

1907 began badly, with a series of illnesses. Both children, in fact, came close to dying. Borys had measles, followed by lung trouble; the baby a very serious attack of whooping-cough. And Conrad's own gout was tormenting. For convalescence, he thought of Champel, which had proved so favourable before to his own health. When various immediate crises had been passed, the family removed there. The place worked wonders, and all were soon in health. At the beginning of August they returned to Pent Farm, and then removed to Someries, near Luton in Bedfordshire, which was to be their home for more than a year.

The effect of such chequered months was to cause Conrad to abandon *Chance* altogether for the time, and to take up a new theme, more in line with *The Secret Agent* than anything else he had done. This was his Russian novel, at first called *Razumov*, after its hero, but changed later to *Under Western Eyes*. The idea rose from a conversation he had had at Geneva more than ten years before. Again it dealt with revolution—and betrayal, and it ranks with his best work.

In the autumn, while he was writing it, Ford Madox Ford started *The English Review*. Conrad took a keen interest in the venture. He had interrupted *Nostromo* to write *The Mirror of the Sea* for his own distraction. He now broke off from *Under Western Eyes* to write some personal reminiscences for Ford. These were afterwards to appear in *A Personal Record*. They deal largely with his early years in Poland and his life at Marseilles, and give some account of his experiences as a writer.

In 1909 another move occurred, this time to Alding-

G

ton, near Hythe in Kent, a county which Conrad always
liked. But he found the place uncongenial, and was soon
saying to Galsworthy that 'this hole is growing more
odious to me every day.' He was, none the less, writing
well. From this time dates 'The Secret Sharer,' one of
the best stories relating to the *Otago*, his first command.
'I am aware of a marked mental improvement,' he said.
'Only two years of no worse health would put me
right with the world. But I daren't hope—and yet I am
unwilling to despair.'

By January 1910 he had finished *Under Western Eyes*,
but then, for the next two months, he was in bed,
suffering tortures from gout. 'I long for a clear run for
my work, you understand,' he wrote to Galsworthy:
'No gouty obstacles—a clear twelve months. I've never
had that in all my writing life.'

At the end of June he migrated to Capel House,
Orlestone, near Ashford, which was to anchor him, as
much as any place ever could, for nearly ten years. Here
he wrote a series of stories, including 'Freya of the
Seven Isles,' one of the most moving and tragic of all
the Malayan series.

It was at this time that the *New York Herald*, at the
instigation of his friend and admirer Sir Hugh Clifford,
whose distinguished service in Malaya had made him an
unmatched authority on that land, made an offer to buy
his work in advance. The immediate result was to make
him resume work on his abandoned novel, *Chance*, now
some five years set aside. Pushing ahead with energy,
he had completed it by the spring of 1912. It was to
prove itself a landmark in his career.

There followed that macabre story of the Peninsula,
'The Inn of the Two Witches'; another Malayan piece,
'Because of the Dollars'; and two newspaper articles on

the loss of the *Titanic*, which, as so often with Conrad's
non-political journalism, suffered from too much immedi-
acy. To produce his best work, rumination was a
necessity.

His next major task, one which occupied him until the
end of June 1914, was *Victory*. Meanwhile, thanks to
the immense efforts at publicity and 'promotion' exerted
by his American publisher, Mr. F. N. Doubleday, *Chance*
was made into a great popular success in America. This
fact eventually had such repercussions in this country
that Conrad's financial difficulties were over, once for
all. For the rest of his life, he never needed to be
anxious on the score of money, though he would not
have been a Korzeniowski had not his ideas continued
to outpace his means of achieving them. He always lived
in as great a style as he could afford; but the days of
1905 when he had been grateful to his friends for getting
him a modest grant from the Civil List were now happily
over. *Chance*, though good, is not among his greatest
books. *Victory*, its successor, certainly is.

About the time that *Victory* was finished, Conrad and
his family had a pressing invitation to visit Poland. He
dearly wished his sons to see his native land, and accepted with pleasure. On 24 July 1914 they started for
Cracow, by the Hamburg route. In the light of history
it seems a preposterous time to have chosen, but it must
be recalled that Western Europe had for several years
been in a state of tension, as it was in the years immediately before 1939. Conrad would have argued that the
crises of 1914 were as likely to dissolve at the last
moment as those of other years.

They had hardly arrived in Poland before Austria
mobilized. After 1 August their retreat was cut off: and
so it came about that Conrad saw the opening of the

conflict, which was at last to liberate his country, from within Poland itself.

His immediate anxiety was, naturally, how to return. Thanks to the efforts of the American Ambassador in Vienna, Mr. Frederick C. Penfield, he and the family were enabled to reach the Austrian capital by car, arriving early in October. They were only just in time to escape internment for the rest of the war. From Austria they made their way to Milan, thence to Genoa, and home by a Dutch ship returning from Java.

His first work completed after the outbreak of the war, *The Shadow Line*, is not only one of the best stories he ever wrote: it has its particular bearing on his personal life, for it is the story of a dark crisis, surmounted after great hazards.

V

The Shadow Line, like *Victory*, was in Conrad's best manner. At the beginning of 1915 he turned away from fiction to record his impressions of Poland in a series of newspaper articles, later included in *Notes on Life and Letters*. His eldest son now joined the Army; his wife's health remained precarious, and although he was relieved of grosser material cares, the fact seemed merely another touch of irony. ' "The Planter of Malata," ' he wrote to Galsworthy about one of his lesser stories, 'earned eight times as much as "Youth," six times as much as "Heart of Darkness." It makes one sick.' It was left to the future to redress the balance, to recognize the merit of the earlier works, to leave the less good less read.

After writing other stories, none of the highest merit, Conrad took the advice of his literary agent, Mr. J. B. Pinker, and began to revise and rewrite *The Rescue*, laid aside many years before.

The world conflict, both for personal and wider reasons, occupied him deeply. Of the attitude of this country he never had a moment's doubt. 'If England comes into the war,' he wrote just before the Declaration, 'then, no matter who may want to make peace at the end of six months at the cost of right and justice, England will keep on fighting for years if necessary. You may reckon on that.

' "What, even alone?" asked somebody across the room.

'I said: "Yes, even alone. But if things go as far as that, England will not be alone." ' Conrad added:

'I think that at that moment I must have been inspired.'

Too old to serve at sea, too frail in health to engage in continuous war-work, he accepted in 1916 the invitation of the Admiralty to visit naval stations, and to put his impressions on record. He visited Edinburgh, Liverpool and Great Yarmouth. He was attached for a time to a special-service anti-submarine vessel, the *Ready*, working in the North Sea area.

Then, and for long after, ill-informed people were critical of the part the Navy were playing in the war. As usual, his own discernment was acute. 'I don't like that sort of inclination to spur on the Admiralty which I seem to detect in the public mind,' he wrote to his friend Christopher Sandeman. 'Spur on—to what? This war (like every other) has to be won on land. The Navy has been playing—*is* playing—its part as well as ever it has played it before. If the public mind wants a great fleet victory I can't for the life of me see what material effect such a victory could have. Of course it would buck us up morally; it would be a great occasion for cheering all along the line. But the important consideration is that it would not demoralize Germany to

any appreciable extent.   For they know and admit their
inferiority on that point.'

VI

Accustomed though the country grew to war and
slaughter during the Furious Forties of the present century, it is difficult, for those who do not themselves
remember the atmosphere of the time, to realize the
agony of those who had sons and husbands serving on
the Western Front between 1914 and 1918. In the spate
of books which have since appeared, the horror has been
fully recorded. Expectation of life for fit young men was
a few weeks only; and the Conrads, with their elder
son at the front, shared the tension to the full. Borys
did not escape scot-free, but he survived. Conrad's own
fear of insolvency, once for all relieved by success, had
been followed by war anxiety, with the accompaniment
of a constant feeling that his creative flow would dry
up. But fears at last dissolved before facts.

Much of Conrad's energy in the later part of the war,
and the years following immediately upon it, was
engaged with dramatic versions of his stories and novels.
They caused him toil, and did not add to his stature as a
writer. His plays are craftsmanly, but they are a waste
of effort which could have been employed better upon
straightforward narrative. Nor did *The Arrow of Gold*, a
novel which he published in 1919, and the first which
he entirely dictated, further his reputation. In it, he
harked back to his days at Marseilles, and he contrived
to create a 'mysterious beauty,' in the character of Rita.
But Rita partakes more of mystery than of life. There is
much personal history embedded in the book, but of all
his novels it is the least satisfying and the least satis-

factory. It almost deserves the sentence which a flippant reader once used, after finishing a novel, that he had 'been listening to a performance on the Conrad.'

The performance which would most have pleased the author at this time would have been a novel about Napoleon. The idea had long attracted him, and indeed his first post-war excursion was by car through France to Marseilles, thence to Corsica, where he hoped to sketch the background. To motor was, for him, always an exciting mode of travel; he had long been fond of cars, and in his last years attained the splendour of a Daimler once owned by the Duke of Connaught. The French trip was pleasant, but the theme remained refractory. 'I can't get my teeth into the novel,' he wrote to Galsworthy. 'I am tired of thinking.'

He decided to break off what he was doing and to write a short story. The material took charge of him, and resulted in *The Rover*. It is quite the most assured and perfect of his later books. Many have noted the 'homing instinct' which pervades it. Jean Peyrol, its hero, an old 'brother of the coast', has returned to his native land with a small fortune in gold, intending that his last few years shall be in peace. He becomes involved in the affairs of an isolated group of people in the lonely farm called Escampobar. The story resolves itself into a study of the effects of the French Revolution upon the handful who inhabit the place. The crisis comes not in the way Peyrol expects; for he actually finds himself able to outwit the blockading squadron under Lord Nelson, off Toulon, and sacrifices his life in a splendid gesture of fidelity.

Conrad dedicated the story to his future biographer, and it was, indeed, the most sustained and perhaps the most enduring tribute to France he ever paid. Artistically, it is almost flawless, and he could not possibly have complained of its reception, except perhaps in the shrillness, which must certainly have prejudiced more than one potential reader of the rising generation against it.

Conrad was indeed now hailed everywhere as a master, a writer for whom the only possible living comparison was with Thomas Hardy. 'One opens his pages,' said Virginia Woolf in a beautiful tribute, 'and feels as Helen must have felt when she looked in her glass and realized that, do what she would, she could never in any circumstances pass for a plain woman.'

He endured a minor set-back in the failure of the dramatic version of *The Secret Agent* on the London stage; on the other hand the visit he paid to America in April 1923, at the invitation of his American publisher, was a personal triumph. The United States was one of the comparatively few countries he did not already know at first hand. Those who knew his novels best could have found in them, without difficulty, passages which might have touched the susceptibilities of Americans; but from first to last he received a welcome which at once surprised, moved and exhausted him.

He sailed from Glasgow in the *Tuscania*, Captain David Bone. With him went the captain's brother Muirhead, then as now celebrated as draughtsman and etcher, and one of the best recorders of the war at sea which was lately over. The pair got on famously. Their cabins communicated. 'Our cabin steward is an amiable old fraud,' wrote Conrad to his wife. Experience came well to his aid. 'He has taken Muirhead in completely —but I have talked straight to him this morning at 7 a.m. and we are now on terms of a strict understanding as to service and tips.'

It is only lately (1949) that Captain (now Sir David)

Bone, in an instructive introduction to *Four Tales* by Conrad in the Worlds Classics, has given his own account of this voyage, as well as a reminiscence of how urgent Conrad had been, years before, that in spite of the success of *The Brassbounder*, his younger friend should not forsake the sea for writing—as a way of life. 'Never "leave the ship," ' he had written in 1910, 'least of all for literature.' David Bone, he perceived at once, would write too well, as indeed he did himself, to support life as adequately from the pen as by service in merchantmen.

Sir David's impression that Conrad regarded the officers of the *Tuscania* as 'an administrative force rather than as the commanding officers he had known' is fully borne out by Conrad's own letters. He was silent, interested, somewhat puzzled perhaps at the way a modern transatlantic liner was run; and although he felt the Captain himself to be a true sea-brother, steam, as usual, left him with a certain distaste.

Conrad stayed some six weeks at Oyster Bay, New York, but in spite of many requests to appear in public and to give lectures, he only consented to give one reading. For this he chose *Victory*: an interesting choice, and a shrewd one, since this novel was in fact the last Conrad had published equal to his own best work.

The reading was to an audience of about fifty people at the house of Mrs. Arthur Curtiss James, in New York. 'A most fashionable affair,' he wrote to Mr. Richard Curle on 11 May, '—and what is more, a real success. I gave a talk and readings . . . one hour and a quarter, with an ovation at the end. They were most attentive. Laughs at proper places and snuffles at the last when I read the whole chapter of Lena's death. It was a great social function, and people fought for invitations. I made it clearly understood from the first that I was not doing this sort of thing for money. This gave my visit to U.S. a particular character about which the press spoke out. . . .'

Soon after the reading he motored from New York to Boston, and on 2 June he sailed for England on the *Majestic*, his last sea passage of any consequence. This liner was then one of the largest afloat, but her size did not impress him, and the voyage lacked the companionship which had made that on the *Tuscania* so worth while.

In the July and August of 1923 he was at his house at Bishopsbourne, near Canterbury, working intermittently on *Suspense*, which was to remain unfinished, Napoleon as ever eluding him. In September he visited Havre with his wife and his younger son John. It was the last time he crossed the sea.

The final year of his life, during which he was offered and declined a knighthood, he devoted to *Suspense*, to some essays, and to considering a volume of memories and impressions which would have supplemented *The Mirror of the Sea*. It was spent at home, although he was planning yet another move. There are signs of tiredness in his writing, but it did not appear to his friends that his health, never robust, was worse than usual. At the beginning of August 1924 he went to see over a new house, in company with Mr. Curle, and was forced to turn back, as he felt ill. On the 3rd, he had a very severe heart attack, from which he did not recover. He died at sixty-six, young enough for there to have been general expectation of perhaps a decade of writing still before him.

It would be an understatement to say that his death was a shock. It was a blow. Many who did not know him felt it personally, just as they had felt that of Byron a century before. His appeal had been to the heart, sailor-fashion, as well as to the intelligence. Tribute was universal.

The news came to the present writer when at sea, in the liner *Andania*, then making her way across the western ocean. It took the form of a laconic wireless message. The bouquets followed, and they all emphasized, what was true, that Conrad had died at the height of his fame. That fact, pleasing enough in its way, aroused general speculation as to what permanent qualities were to be found in his work. Not many ventured to prophesy, but among them was an elderly chief officer. 'They can think what they like about his other books,' he said. 'To me, he'll always be the man who saw McWhirr through that typhoon! I fancy he'll live by that.' The view was by no means singular.

Conrad is buried in the cemetery at Canterbury, in the county he had long loved. He once spoke of the best friend to his work as being 'the cool green light on the fields.' Restless as he was by nature, Kent had held him in life for fifteen years: first Aldington, then Orlestone, and, for the last five, Bishopsbourne. He is now hers for ever.

The stone on his grave bears his Polish name, and that quotation from Spenser which he had used on the title-page of *The Rover*:

Sleep after toyle, port after stormie seas,
Ease after warre, death after life, does greatly please.

_____

GREATER NOVELS

VISITORS to Portsmouth may, if they are so minded, see over Nelson's *Victory*. There she lies, an impressive tribute to nautical research, and a monument to past glory. Every detail is of interest, down to the leathern fire-buckets which belong to her prime, the iron cannon balls which are rubbed over every day with a slightly oily rag, and the chain pump, the only mechanical contrivance on board. She is perfect, but lifeless, like a steamship with cold boilers. For what made the *Victory* herself was not this devoted care for incidentals, but the heterogeneous, imperfect men who once manned her, the immense spread of sail which they controlled and which has disappeared for ever; above all, the genius of successive men who flew their flag in her, of whom the greatest will never be forgotten.

It is with somewhat similar feelings to those which arise in a survey of the *Victory* that a writer views the undoubted necessity of analysis. He may prose away, explain, quote, theorize about his author, but all the while the life of the affair will be apt to evade him. For the beauty of examination, if indeed it should rise to it, is a cold enough thing. Analysis sometimes misses the heart of the matter, and in truth the best comment upon all who are of classical rank may be said to lie in the injunction—Read their books; and if the magic prove elusive no manner of explaining how and why it is done will be an adequate introduction.

Conrad, like Henry James, wrote valuable prefaces or 'Author's Notes' to collected editions of his work. They were shorter than James's, and far less involved, but were composed with as much care and threw as much (or as little) light on the actual processes of creation. If such processes are ever explicable, explanation is never enough. In fact, the self-revelation is enjoyable chiefly by writers and scholars; and the writers would often be more happily engaged in creating than in trying to learn from the *obiter dicta* let fall by fellow-craftsmen.

'Watching a coast as it slips by the ship is like thinking about an enigma,' runs a passage in 'Heart of Darkness.' 'There it is before you—smiling, frowning, irritating, grand, mean, insipid or savage, and always mute with an air of whispering, come and find out.' The observation is equally true in considering an author of stature. Scene after scene is evoked, and the reader, excited or lulled by the impression conveyed, is often aware that it is only the fringe that slips so colourfully past his eye. When it has gone, when the ship has left the land away in the darkness, and the reader has turned the last page, it is the echoes which matter. It was Conrad himself who said: 'A work that aspires, however humbly, to the condition of art should carry its justification in every line.' Thereafter, only signposts should be necessary.

Readers of Conrad will either have been captivated by him, or they will have been left cold. He provokes extremes. For those who have been left cold, enormous persuasion will be required to cause them to return to him. If they have come under his spell, they will have made their choice as to which of his novels and stories they consider to be of the highest importance. They will be prepared if necessary to defend them against all comers.

Conrad wrote no less than eleven full-length novels, besides his two collaborations with Ford Madox Ford, and his unfinished *Suspense*, which was conceived, though not, alas, executed, on a great scale. He also wrote a number of stories, such as *Typhoon* and *The Nigger of the 'Narcissus,'* which rank almost as short novels. The novels which will here be treated as 'greater' are *Lord Jim* (1900), which may be said to reach the category only by a narrow margin; *Nostromo* (1904); *The Secret Agent* (1907); *Under Western Eyes* (1911); *Victory* (1915) and *The Rover* (1923). Stories as long as *The Nigger* and as short as 'The Inn of the Two Witches' will be separately considered, as belonging to the slightly different art of the *conte*.

LORD JIM (1900)

Conrad, always acutely sensitive to criticism, was once surprised by hearing that a lady had expressed the view that *Lord Jim* was 'all so morbid.' The shock was explicable, since it is not a comment which would occur to most readers. 'I wonder whether she was a European?' he inquires in his Preface. 'In any case, no Latin temperament would have perceived anything morbid in the acute consciousness of lost honour.'

Lost—and redeemed in full: that is the theme of *Lord Jim*. It is not to be wondered at that so appealing a subject should have won the book relative popularity. A tale with a moral has always had the likelihood of ready acceptance in England, particularly if clothed in such majesty of language as Conrad could exercise.

His hero, an officer of the merchant marine, had

'jumped into an everlasting deep hole,' or so it seemed. He had, in fact, leaped in the darkness from what he thought to be a sinking steamer, the *Patna*. She had been crowded with pilgrims, for whom there were no boats. The other officers of the vessel were by any professional standard dishonourable and cowardly, but Lord Jim found himself inevitably sharing in their infamy. As for his actual conduct, 'there was not the thickness of a sheet of paper between the right and wrong of his affair.' He thought, when he jumped, that the *Patna* could not last more than a few seconds longer.

In the boat, the officers who have left her believe they see the lights of the ship disappear. Jim himself even fancies he hears cries in the water. In fact, the *Patna* continues to drift, and is later found by a French gun-boat, which tows her to port. Jim, alone of the officers, feels it his duty to face a full examination.

The whole process of investigation is described in detail by one of Conrad's narrators who, under one guise or another, appear in so many of his stories. Through the medium of this same narrator, in this case Marlow, Jim is given the chance to turn his back upon his haunted life, the 'enticing, disenchanting and enslaving life at sea.' He is sent to a trading area in a little-known part of the East. He rules his far-away native community with skill, enterprise and justice. He is honoured, loved —and betrayed. A party of white men at length pene-trate to his secret world, and, although Jim has given his word that if allowed to leave the country unharmed they will themselves take no life, they in fact do so, and Jim feels it necessary to forfeit his own in expiation of their perfidy.

In the same Preface already quoted, Conrad says that 'when this novel first appeared in book form a notion got about that I had been bolted away with.' The accusation was that a short story had been puffed out into a novel. 'The truth of the matter is,' he continues, 'that my first thought was of a short story, concerned only with the pilgrim ship episode; nothing more. After writing a few pages, however, I became for some reason discontented and I laid them aside for a time. I didn't take them out of the drawer until the late Mr. William Blackwood suggested I should give something again to his magazine. It was only then that I perceived that the pilgrim ship episode was a good starting-point for a free and wandering tale.'

Although 'free and wandering' in detail, and to some extent in method, *Lord Jim* is a novel of three very distinct plots: Jim's time in the *Patna*; his interrogation by the shipping authorities, with the self-exile and spiritual torment which follow; finally, the colour, drama, and success of a new life. Such diversity of narrative interest is justified if the parts coalesce, as in fact they do.

Lord Jim marks a great advance in assurance, in depth of feeling, and in the quality of its prose upon Conrad's earliest novels, *Almayer's Folly* and *An Outcast of the Islands*, with which some of its background may be compared. He had already, in for instance *The Nigger of the 'Narcissus'* (1897) and 'An Outpost of Progress' (1898) published work of great power, and his next considerable novel, *Nostromo* (1904), was to be his most ambitious. He was, in fact, striking his finest form. Judged by this, *Lord Jim* is not wholly successful, but by any other standard it deserves the respectful consideration it is usually given.

H

NOSTROMO (1904)

Conrad's novels and stories, by reason of their background, tend to group themselves into series. There are the Malayan tales, with which he began his career; there are those about the high seas; a third series whose background is France; and some studies of revolutionaries. But one novel, his longest and 'most anxiously meditated,' stands quite alone. It is *Nostromo*, a book which is as far removed from *Lord Jim* as that novel is from a conventional love-story. In Conrad's own work it had no direct forerunners, and a successor, by his hand or that of any other, would have been unlikely. For Conrad created not merely a number of highly individual characters, but a complete political state. Costaguana, the place in question, is so convincing in its details that when, after finishing it, one re-reads that passage in the preface where the author speaks of his Antonia 'moving in the dimness of the great cathedral, saying a short prayer at the tomb of the first and last Cardinal-Archbishop of Sulaco, standing absorbed in filial devotion before the monument of Don José Avellanos, and, with a lingering, tender, faithful glance at the medallion-memorial to Martin Decoud, going out serenely into the sunshine of the Plaza with her upright carriage and her white head; a relic of the past disregarded by men awaiting impatiently the Dawns of other New Eras, the coming of more Revolutions'—when one reads this, the conclusion is irresistible that *Nostromo* is in the fullest sense a living book. The characters seem to possess an independent existence. The reader is apt to remember them as he might a group of friends in a far-away community which he has at some time known well. They will develop, they will grow older, but the pattern of their lives will continue much the same. In fact, the knowledge acquired about them will remain valid even if chance never again allows the opportunity to pick up threads once followed with affection. It is a quality which belongs to few books, and is one of the rarest to which a novel may attain. *Nostromo* is in no possible sense an easy book, but it is so compelling, once the reader has surrendered to it, that it is as hard to forget as is an outstanding performance of a great play. It is Conrad's most sustained effort as an artist. No narrator or intermediary distracts the directness of what he relates. Like that coveted ore, the gaining of which is one of its principal themes, it contains 'an incorruptible metal, that can be trusted to keep its value for ever'—or for at least as long as men and women continue to be interested in English fiction of a serious kind. Conrad began his first book on the margins of a novel by Flaubert. In *Nostromo*, to quote a most valuable study by Dr. F. R. Leavis, he is 'fully conscious of French initiation, and of fellowship in craft' with that austere master.

'I will take the liberty to point out,' Conrad says in one of his later letters, 'that silver is the pivot of the moral and material events, affecting the lives of everybody in the tale. That this was my deliberate purpose there can be no doubt. I struck the first note of my intention in the unusual form which I gave to the title of the first part, by calling it "The Silver of the Mine." '

The incorruptibility of silver is contrasted ironically with its disintegrating effects upon the entire life of his republic, and upon many of the people in his story. We see revolution, of which 'the fundamental causes were the same as ever, rooted in the political immaturity of the people, in the indolence of the upper classes and the mental darkness of the lower'; we see Nostromo (not so much a conventional hero as a character who helps to give the story unity of person) as a man whose well-being is wholly dependent on the effect he makes upon other people. Nostromo's entire existence is trans-formed, not for the better, by the fact that he has successfully made away with a whole lighter-load of silver in bars. We see the Gould Concession, managing the Great San Tomé mine upon which the economy of the country turns, become, after swift changing fortune, the rallying centre for all who look for peace and order. The end of the book shows a republic in which good administration and material interests seem to have triumphed. Progress is 'forging ahead.' American capital has cast its massive shadow upon affairs. 'We shall run the world's business whether it likes it or not,' says the millionaire Holroyd, in a spirit of justified pro-phecy. 'The world can't help it—and neither can we, I guess.'

The Concession has indeed triumphed over all hazards, but with Conrad's invariable irony he shows it as becom-ing the focus of hate for workers and indigent alike, a symbol of oppression for such idealists and defenders of the spirit who still live in the capital, Sulaco. It has defeated all opposition, and in sacrificing himself body and mind to its interests, even the mercurial English-man, Charles Gould, a gallant, romantic, and on the whole sympathetic character, has (though he scarcely perceives it) sacrificed the personal happiness of his gracious wife.

As he says, so it comes about. 'What is wanted here is law, good faith, order, security. Anyone can declaim about these things, but I pin my faith to material inter-ests. Only let material interests once get a firm footing, and they are bound to impose the conditions on which alone they can continue to exist. That's how your money-making is justified here in the face of lawlessness and disorder. It is justified because the security which it demands must be shared with an oppressed people. A better justice will come afterwards. That's your ray of hope.' After capital, a form of Marxism? It is, at any rate, one deduction from the passage that Conrad perceived an inevitable sequence, though not the bitter implications time is teaching us.

Martin Decoud, another character central to the story, shares in Nostromo's exploit with the lighter-load of silver. He is sophisticated, intellectual, dilettante, a sceptic with 'no faith in anything except the truth of his own sensations.' In Antonia Avellanos he finds a woman worthy of the passion of a better man; for when faced with himself, after Nostromo has left him alone with the treasure they have buried on the lonely islet of Great Isabel, his inner resources fail him utterly. 'After three days of waiting for the sight of some human face,' says Conrad, 'Decoud caught himself entertaining a doubt of his own individuality. It had merged into the world of cloud and water, of natural forces and forms of nature. . . . Both his intelligence and his passion were swallowed up easily in the great unbroken solitude of waiting without faith.' Unable to bear his own society longer than a few days, believing that Nostromo will never return, Decoud, who is a fugitive from revolution, kills himself. Although unexpected, the turn of event as Conrad describes it has an air of inevitability. Needless as his death was, in view of Nostromo's later return, the reader feels that he could have taken no other course. 'I be nothing,' says a character in one of Mr. T. F. Powys's novels, 'and I mid hang myself.' So it is with Decoud.

The open, vain and resourceful Nostromo has a counterpart in Georgio Viola, an old Garibaldino with whom he has lived. As Dr. Leavis says, Viola is almost self-sufficient, not, like Nostromo, through vanity, but by reason of his libertarian idealism, the disinterestedness of which is above all question. 'He represents with monumental massiveness the heroic age of the liberal faith.'

At least two other characters command attention. They are Dr. Monygham, a man who is universally disliked and distrusted, but who, for all his self-contempt and cynicism, holds to an exacting ideal of conduct. He perceives the truth about the Goulds. His loyalty is to Mrs. Gould, who although she is the perfect wife to the public man has, he perceives, an inner integrity which will be unshaken by reversal of fortune. The other outstanding personality is Captain Mitchell, a port official trained in the British merchant service. He is sane almost to the point of stupidity. When menaced by the unleashed forces of revolution, all he can think about is that a gang of ruffians have stolen his presentation pocket-chronometer. He is set upon its return with such complete singleness of mind, such oblivion to the larger events around him, that he succeeds in his immediate end. He is released from the violent restraint which had been put upon him, and his precious property is restored.

So packed, detailed and vivid is the story, that to analyse it as thoroughly as it deserves would be to précis it. There are no superfluities, amply planned though it is. Its moral, implicit in the story, has particular bearing upon the present time. There is the contrast drawn between a disintegrated society, in which few are happy but all are 'free,' and the constriction—and security— which follows behind the establishment of large-scale industrial production. Silver—the very metal is in a sense second-rate: and that, Conrad seems to imply, is the essence of the case. The choice is between freedom with squalor, and order with slavery. And the order, as he insists with many subtle touches, always comes with a flavour of idealism, however faint, while freedom cannot escape its consequences of violence and unreason.

Most of all to be remarked is the marvellous illusion of the book. While writing it, Conrad 'lived' in Costaguana, and more particularly in Sulaco, 'standing beneath snow-clad Higuerota.' This was so in all but a grossly literal sense, and his power is such that he carries his readers with him. His writing was never more splendid, even in his later years, when experience had added to its flexibility.

'On crossing the imaginary line drawn from Punta Mala to Azuera,' runs a passage at the opening of the book, 'the ships from Europe bound to Sulaco lose at once the strong breezes of the ocean. They become the prey of capricious airs that play with them for thirty hours at a stretch sometimes. Before them the head of the calm gulf is filled on most days of the year by a great body of motionless and opaque clouds. On the rare clear mornings another shadow is cast upon the sweep of the gulf. The dawn breaks high behind the towering and serrated wall of the Cordillera, a clear-cut vision of dark peaks rearing their steep slopes on a lofty pedestal of forest rising from the very edge of the shore. Amongst them the white head of Higuerota rises majestically upon the blue. Bare clusters of enormous rocks sprinkle with tiny black dots the smooth dome of snow.'

Crossing that 'imaginary line' with Conrad, in 'willing suspension of disbelief,' is the fullest adventure he can offer as a novelist, and the most rewarding. It is a journey bewildering in its variety, seldom direct in its progress, and the diversions are not often light-hearted. But when it is remembered that it was written in the plum-cake reign of Edward VII, and that its bearing upon some of the more pressing problems of the present day could scarcely be closer, it must be a matter of astonishment that it has not had wider recognition. Small wonder at Conrad's bitterness at his lack of popular audience. It is the penalty of many artists to be ahead of their age, and it would be hard to come upon a work of fiction in which this fact is more apparent. It will never, perhaps, be a general favourite even among Conrad's staunch admirers, for its effect is in total too austere. *Nostromo* is touched with something of the lofty chill of the peak of Higuerota, but that it is in every respect remarkable, that it deserves to take rank with the greatest novels of the English language, is not an extravagant claim.

THE SECRET AGENT (1907)

'The inception of *The Secret Agent*,' says Conrad, 'followed immediately on a two years' period of intense absorption in the task of writing that remote novel *Nostromo*, with its far-off Latin-American atmosphere: and the profoundly personal *The Mirror of the Sea*. The first an intense creative effort on what I suppose will always be my largest canvas'—he wrote in 1920—'the second an unreserved attempt to unveil for a moment the profounder intimacies of the sea and the formative influences of nearly half my lifetime.'

Change was what he sought, and the transition from fiction to reminiscence was, apparently, not enough.

And just as the origin of *Nostromo* was a vague story he had once heard as a young man in the Caribbean, of a sailor 'who was supposed to have stolen single-handed a lighter-load of silver, somewhere on the Tierra Firme seaboard during the troubles of a revolution,' so did *The Secret Agent* begin 'in the shape of a few words uttered by a friend in a casual conversation about anarchists, or rather anarchistic activities. . . .' The friend was Ford.

Someone, it was then well remembered, had once tried to destroy Greenwich Observatory with a bomb. He had merely succeeded in blowing himself to pieces, leaving it to time, neglect and the hand of a more competent enemy to bring to the place an air of ruination. 'The man concerned,' said the friend, 'was half an idiot. His sister committed suicide afterwards.' It was that sentence which set Conrad thinking. 'Of the illuminating quality there could be no doubt whatever,' he remarks. From such desultory wreckage he set to work to build up the sordid world of the Verlocs, set within the greater world of a London which still held the flavour of Dickens. Once the idea had seized him, it was a question mainly of 'attending to my business. In the matter of all my books,' he added, 'I have always attended to my business. I have attended to it with complete surrender. And this statement is not a boast. I could not have done otherwise. It would have bored me too much to make-believe.'

'*The Secret Agent*—a Simple Tale,' he called it with conscious irony; for although, as in *Nostromo*, the narrative is straightforward, in careful building up of plot it yields to none among his longer stories, and the characters themselves are anything but transparent.

'The way of even the most justifiable revolutions,' he

says at a critical point in the book, 'is prepared by
personal impulses disguised into creeds.' History affords
much evidence to support this remark. 'In their own
way,' he adds elsewhere, 'the most ardent of revolutionaries are doing nothing but seeking for peace in
common with the rest of mankind—the peace of soothed
vanity, of satisfied appetites, or perhaps of appeased
conscience.' Of Mrs. Verloc, one of the principal
characters of *A Secret Agent*, he says most aptly: 'She felt
profoundly that things do not stand much looking into.'
She typifies the sane, in contrast to the savagely unbalanced forces into which her life has brought her.
For the secret agent himself, Verloc, acts on behalf of a
power, one of whose diplomatic representatives in
London says: 'The general leniency of the judicial procedure here, and the utter absence of all repressive
measures, are a scandal to Europe. What is wished for
just now is the accentuation of the unrest—of the
fermentation which undoubtedly exists. . . .' Again,
as with *Nostromo*, it is with a shock that one considers
the year in which the book was published.

The setting of the story is fittingly sordid, and it may
be noted that such a milieu is seldom met with elsewhere
in Conrad. Much of the action takes place in 'one of
those grimy brick houses which existed in large quan-
tities before the era of reconstruction dawned upon
London. The shop was a square box of a place, with
the front glazed in small panes. In the daytime the door
remained closed; in the evening it stood discreetly but
suspiciously ajar. The window contained photographs of
more or less undressed dancing girls; nondescript pack-
ages in wrappers like patent medicines; closed yellow
paper envelopes, very flimsy, and marked two-and-six
in heavy black figures; a few numbers of ancient French

comic publications hung across a string as if to dry; a dingy blue china bowl, a casket of black wood, bottles of marking ink, and rubber stamps; a few books, with titles hinting at impropriety; a few apparently old copies of newspapers, badly printed, with titles like *The Torch*, *The Gong*—rousing titles. And the two gas-jets inside the panes were always turned low, either for economy's sake, or for the sake of the customers.'

With the scene set thus, no wonder the professional 'realist' writers of the time pricked up their ears. Conrad could set the scene. Could he keep it up?

The answer was not long in doubt. He could and did. He had an unusual plot: the screw being put upon his secret agent by a particularly odious type of official, the Mr. Vladimir whose opinion of the British legal system was so uncomplimentary. It is possible to insult even a secret agent, keeping a disreputable shop in the East End to serve him as a blind, and Mr. Vladimir proceeds to do it. He insists that something terrific must be done.

' "It will cost money," Mr. Verloc said, by a sort of instinct.

' "That cock won't fight," Mr. Vladimir retorted, with an amazingly genuine English accent. "You'll get your screw every month, and no more till something happens. And if nothing happens very soon you won't even get that. What's your ostensible occupation? What are you supposed to live by?"

' "I keep a shop," answered Mr. Verloc.

' "A shop! What sort of shop?"

' "Stationery, newspapers. My wife——"

' "Your what?" interrupted Mr. Vladimir in his guttural Central Asian tones.

' "My wife," Mr. Verloc raised his husky voice slightly. "I am married."

' "That be damned for a yarn," exclaimed the other in unfeigned astonishment. "Married! And you a professed anarchist too! What is this confounded nonsense? But I suppose it's merely a matter of speaking. Anarchists don't marry. It's well known. They can't. It would be apostasy." '

It is possible, in this passage and others, to detect a very slight note of strain in Conrad's dialogue. It is almost too perfect. Actually, Vladimir had disturbed his agent in every fibre of his being. Hitherto he had been trusted.

' "There isn't a murdering plot for the last eleven years that I haven't had my finger in at the risk of my life," he says. "There's scores of these revolutionaries I've sent off, with their bombs in their blamed pockets, to get themselves caught on the frontier. The old Baron knew what I was worth to his country. And here suddenly a swine comes along—an ignorant, overbearing swine," ' who expects a miracle.

Vladimir has not only asked the near-impossible, but he has made insinuations about Verloc's wife. Just how real a character Winnie Verloc is soon becomes apparent. She accepts; she works; she does not ask questions. Hers has, perhaps, been a strange marriage and, as she says, 'Obviously it may be good for me not to know too much.' Nevertheless, she has made life tolerable.

Winnie has a mother, a somewhat Dickensian figure who shares with her daughter an utterly unselfish concern for Stevie, the half-witted son. For his sake, she betakes herself to an almshouse, in a scene which has much of the convincing exaggeration by which Dickens achieves his effects. She does not think it right that Verloc should have more than one useless person in his household.

Winnie thereupon sets out to impress Verloc with Stevie's devotion to him. Stevie must never be felt unwanted. Actually, Winnie could not have done a more fatal thing, for Verloc, who is beginning to grow desperate in the matter of the outrage expected from him, uses Stevie as a means of planting the bomb in Greenwich Park. But things go wrong. Stevie stumbles; a shattering but futile explosion takes place; and the only reason it is ever brought home to the Verloc household is by reason of a label—it is among the surviving fragments—which Winnie has sewn on to her brother's coat to prevent his being lost.

The principal *dénouement* is concerned with Winnie's growing realization of her husband's part in Stevie's death. In the end she murders Verloc, for it is Stevie, not he, who is the mainspring of her life. 'He saw partly on the ceiling and partly on the wall the moving shadow of an arm with a clenched hand holding a carving knife. It flickered up and down. Its movements were leisurely enough for Mr. Verloc to recognize the limb and the weapon. They were leisurely enough for Mr. Verloc to elaborate a plan of defence involving a dash behind the table, and the felling of the woman to the ground with a heavy wooden chair. But they were not leisurely enough to allow Mr. Verloc time to move either hand or foot . . . . Mr. Verloc, the Secret Agent, turning slightly on his side with the force of the blow, expired without stirring a limb, in the muttered sound of the word "Don't" by way of protest.'

Dr. Leavis, without hyperbole, calls the final scene between the Verlocs 'one of the most astonishing triumphs of genius in fiction.' It does not end the book, but Winnie's own death, after she has thrown herself upon the frightened care of a revolutionary, Comrade

Ossipon, who has more than once declared his passion for her, but now quickly deserts her, is felt to be quite as inevitable.

Of the various lesser plots, the most interesting, as helping to illustrate Conrad's own attitude to the world, is that in which the necessary action of the police is followed out, and in particular the rivalry that the incident creates between Chief Inspector Heat ('Why not leave it to Heat?') and his superior, the Assistant Commissioner. This official has, in Heat's eyes, shown a most undesirable interest in the details of the case. ('You, my boy,' thinks Heat, 'don't know your place, and your place won't know you very long, I bet.') Heat has his own brand of morality. He wishes to bring the crime home to Michaelis, a ticket-of-leave man against whom he can without difficulty amass sufficient evidence. For Verloc, who has been put in his way some years before, has been helping to provide him with a valuable amount of information, leading to recognition and promotion. To follow the clues as far as Verloc himself would only destroy a rich store of potential profit. 'A department,' remarks Conrad, 'does not know so much as some of its servants. Being a dispassionate organism, it can never be perfectly informed. It would not be good for its efficiency to know too much.'

Heat, one is made to understand, dislikes revolutionaries in a manner which he could never have felt for thieves, by dealing with whom he has risen to responsibility. He knew where he was with thieves, for whom he had 'a feeling not far removed from affection.' He thought (with some reason) that 'thieving was not a sheer absurdity. It was a form of human industry, perverse indeed, but still an industry exercised in an industrious world; it was work undertaken for the same reason as the work in potteries, in coal mines, in fields, in tool-grinding shops. It was labour, whose practical difference from the other forms of labour consisted in the nature of its risk, which did not lie in ankylosis, or lead-poisoning, or fire-damp, or gritty dust, but in what may be briefly defined in its own special phraseology as "Seven years hard." Chief-Inspector Heat was, of course, not insensible to the gravity of moral differences. But neither were the thieves he had been looking after. They submitted to the severe sanctions of a morality familiar to Chief-Inspector Heat with a certain resignation. They were his fellow-citizens gone wrong because of imperfect education. . . .'

But when Heat meets the bomb-making 'Professor' in a narrow alley, his sensations are very different. The 'Professor' knows that he cannot be arrested, for he carries with him always the means of destruction for himself and, no doubt, for any intervening instrument of the law. The encounter, therefore, 'did not leave behind with Inspector Heat that satisfactory sense of superiority the members of the police force get from the unofficial but intimate side of their intercourse with the criminal classes, by which the vanity of power is soothed, the vulgar love of domination over our fellow-creatures is flattered as worthily as it deserves.' No: 'The perfect anarchist was not recognized as a fellow-creature by Chief Inspector Heat.'

The same would, as a generality, be true enough of Conrad, as he made apparent both in *The Secret Agent* and *Under Western Eyes*. But there must be one paramount qualification. The Verlocs themselves are as perfectly, even, it may be added, as sympathetically realized as any people he ever created.

There is one more point which distinguishes *The*

Secret Agent from other novels; it includes a sketch of an eminent politician, Sir William Harcourt, the Liberal leader ('Be lucid . . . Spare me details'), which, according to Sir Desmond MacCarthy, is 'the most vivid description of him to be found.' Harcourt figures as Sir Ethelred, the man within whose province such affairs as that of the Greenwich business comes: 'Vast in bulk and stature, with a long white face which, broadened at the base by a big double chin, appeared egg-shaped in the fringe of thin greyish whisker, the great personage appeared an expanding man. Unfortunate from a tailoring point of view, the cross-folds in the middle of a buttoned black coat added to the impression, as if the fastenings of the garment were tried to the utmost. From the head, set upward on a thick neck, the eyes, with puffy lower lids, stared with a haughty droop on each side of a hooked, aggressive nose, nobly salient in the vast pale circumference of the face. A shining silk hat and a pair of worn gloves lying ready on the end of a long table looked expanded, too, enormous.'

The only comparable vignettes to this are in *The Inheritors*; they are none of them so good, and a great many are Ford's.

The final impression of *The Secret Agent* must be one of astonishment that, in stretching beyond his more familiar horizon, Conrad betrayed no shade of unease, fumbling, or lack of purpose. Had he deliberately chosen the way taken by George Moore in, for instance, *A Mummer's Wife*, by Arnold Bennett in *The Old Wives' Tale* and by H. G. Wells (to whom *The Secret Agent* is dedicated) in some of his earlier novels, there can be no doubt that Conrad would have succeeded in building up, had he so wished, an English world as wide in its canvas as it would have been convincing in its detail.

The Secret Agent attracted attention, and later made a remarkable play. All the same, it is a book by which many affectionate readers of Conrad are made uneasy. Tragedy they are prepared for, but not quite so near home. They look for magic, and are presented here with actuality of the most fly-blown kind. Under no circumstances are either *The Secret Agent* or *Under Western Eyes* likely to become popular novels. But in no two books were their author's talents exercised at a higher level, and it is with a feeling of profound respect that his more recent critics have recognized his mastery in a genre different from anything he had attempted before. As if to reinforce the impression, *Under Western Eyes* continues the same sombre mood, in an utterly different setting. It is irresistible to speculate upon Conrad's reputation had he left nothing beside these two books. They could not long have been ignored. What is certain is that he would have attracted an altogether *different* class of reader. For both novels are capable of imitation, and that is a fate which he has otherwise escaped.

UNDER WESTERN EYES (1911)

In Conrad's bibliography, only one, comparatively unimportant book of stories, *A Set of Six*, stands between his bomb-scarred novels of revolution. *The Secret Agent* and *Under Western Eyes* are rightly linked, for they show a similar line of thought and they rank very high in his work. It may be argued that he wrote books which, in their sphere, are the equal of this pair: but only *Nostromo* could be claimed as artistically superior.

Under Western Eyes has a twofold value. It is a story which holds continuous suspense, if not excitement: and

I

it expresses Conrad's true feelings about Russia—feelings of undisguised hatred. To Russia he felt he owed, directly, the death of his parents, and the eclipse of his compatriots. Nothing angered him more than to be compared in any way with even the most distinguished Russian writers.

In the earlier days of the first world war, when Russia was an ally of Great Britain, he viewed her every move with suspicion. 'Political trustworthiness is not born and matured in three days,' he wrote to Hugh Dent in 1917, when news of the Revolution had given hope of new vigour for the Alliance. A little later in the same year he said: 'Russians (nobody would believe me in 1914) are born rotten.' In 1919 he added, in a letter to Sir Hugh Clifford about the Peace Conference: 'The mangy Russian dog having gone mad is now being invited to sit at the Conference table, on British initiative! The thing is inconceivable, but there it is. One asks oneself whether this is idealism, stupidity or hypocrisy? I do not know who are the individuals responsible, but I hope they will get bitten. . . . The issue is simply life and death.'

Such were his thoughts a few years after the publication of *Under Western Eyes*, and they are not irrelevant, since in his Author's Note to that book he describes it 'as an attempt to render not so much the political state as the psychology of Russia itself.'

'The ferocity and imbecility of an autocratic rule,' he said in the same Note, 'rejecting all legality and in fact basing itself upon complete moral anarchism, provokes the no less imbecile and atrocious answer of a purely Utopian revolutionism encompassing destruction by the first means to hand.' That is the broad theme of the story itself, which is interspersed throughout with asides upon the Russian character which do not seem to have lost their validity. 'Cynicism,' he says, 'is the mark of Russian autocracy and of Russian revolt. In its pride of numbers, in its strong pretensions of sanctity, and in the secret readiness to abase itself in suffering, the spirit of Russia is the spirit of cynicism. It informs the declarations of statesmen, the theories of her revolutionists, and the mystic vaticinations of prophets to the point of making freedom look like a form of debauch, and the Christian virtues themselves appear almost indecent.'

'Whenever two Russians come together,' he says again (and it is once more with astonishment that one realizes that he wrote thirty years ago), 'the shadow of autocracy is with them, tingeing their thoughts, their views, their most intimate feelings, their private life, their public utterances—haunting the secret of their silences.'

Gathering himself for what is in effect a summing up of all that he feels about revolution, Conrad makes his narrator, an old teacher of languages of Western origin, say: '. . . In a real revolution—not a simple dynastic change or a mere reform of institutions—in a real revolution the best characters do not come to the front. A violent revolution falls into the hands of narrow-minded fanatics and of tyrannical hypocrites at first. Afterwards comes the turn of all the pretentious intellectual failures of the time. Such are the chiefs and the leaders. You will notice that I have left out the mere rogues. The scrupulous and the just, the noble, humane, and devoted natures; the unselfish and the intelligent may begin a movement—but it passes away from them. They are not the leaders of a revolution. They are its victims: the victims of disgust, of disenchantment—often of remorse. Hopes grotesquely betrayed, ideals caricatured—that is the definition of revolutionary successes. There have been in every revolution hearts broken by such successes.'

*   *   *

Such observations may help to set the scene for what is after all the most direct and sustained political commentary which Conrad ever made. That it was in the form of a story mattered nothing, except that its impact was more immediate and therefore impressive. Moreover, his point of view, here so definite, is never allowed to affect the pace of the narrative or the building up of character.

His convention is unusual. It is that the journal of Razumov, a young Russian, has come into the hands of the 'old teacher of languages,' resident in Switzerland but familiar with Europe generally, who is therefore able to illuminate its events. He himself plays a small part in the story.

Razumov, as a student, is peculiarly alone: 'as lonely in the world as a fish swimming in the sea.' He has reason to believe in some faint interest in him on the part of 'Prince K——' who is possibly his father; but he is severely discouraged from presumption of any sort. He wishes for distinction. 'There was nothing strange in the student Razumov's wish for distinction,' we are told. 'A man's real life is that accorded to him in the thoughts of other men by reason of respect or natural love.'

One day, a particularly odious member of the bureaucracy is killed by a bomb, the assassin escaping. The deed has actually been done by a young man named Haldin, of good family, and of great courage and nobility. Haldin has been drawn to Razumov by a casual though thoughtful sentence or two he has let fall in conversation. Haldin goes to Razumov's room, to the latter's fear and utter disgust, since he now feels himself ruined. Haldin tells Razumov that if he will rouse the peasant Ziemia-nitch, horses can be brought to meet Haldin at mid-night, and so enable him to get away.

Razumov reluctantly goes on the errand, only to find the peasant in a state of drunken stupor. He beats him mercilessly and then goes out into the snow, with, above his head, 'the clear black sky of the northern winter, decorated with the sumptuous fires of the stars.'

He has a vivid vision of Haldin in the snow, but this does not deter him from his next act, which is to go to 'Prince K——' with the full story. Haldin is caught, but neither the fear of death nor torture make him speak another word.

Razumov is in one respect saved, but he is ruined in another; for he has fairly involved himself, and the police have a use for him. There is a creepy scene with a certain Councillor Mikulin, an eminent bureaucrat. Razumov, during his interview, asserts his right 'to retire.' Mikulin appears to turn the idea over in his mind. Razumov insists. Yes, to retire, he repeats. 'Where to?' asks Mikulin softly, and the interview ends.

Razumov, lonelier than ever, is trapped, and is sent by the police to Geneva, to spy among the revolution-aries. Partly by official ingenuity, partly by chance, his reputation has preceded him. It is as the friend, not the betrayer of Haldin.

In Switzerland, he meets Haldin's sister, a beautiful and cultivated girl who has idolized her brother. He falls in love with her. He is, of course, accepted by the other revolutionaries, of whom Conrad gives a most unpleasant picture. The truth gradually emerges; and

having, by confession to Miss Haldin and to the revolutionaries, escaped at last from the worst of that moral
isolation which he has endured so long, Razumov becomes physically derelict by the end of the book, his
ear-drums deliberately burst by a revolutionary leader
of the most odious type, who turns out later to have
been himself 'a traitor, a betrayer, a spy.'

Razumov returns to Russia, where he lives in 'a little
two-roomed wooden house, in the suburb of a very
small town, hiding within the high plank-fence of a
yard overgrown with nettles.' Though crippled and
deaf, he is faithfully tended by a woman, Tekla, whom
he has known in Switzerland, and whose one idea in
life is to find a person to whom she can give herself with
mindless devotion. As a final touch of that irony which
Conrad employed so much, he is even visited in a
friendly way by some of the revolutionaries. 'He is
intelligent,' they say. 'He has ideas . . . he talks so
well.'

'Nations, it may be,' says Conrad, 'have fashioned
their Governments, but the Governments have paid
them back in the same coin. It is unthinkable that any
young Englishman should find himself in Razumov's
situation. . . . He would not have an hereditary and
personal knowledge of the means by which an historical
autocracy represses ideas, guards its power and defends
its existence. By an act of mental extravagance he might
imagine himself arbitrarily thrown into prison, but it
would never occur to him unless he were delirious (and
perhaps not even then) that he could be beaten with
whips as a practical measure either of investigation or of
punishment.'

Since those words were printed, Europe has taken
certain steps backwards, and the gross idea of torture

has assumed a new meaning and threat, even to many 'young Englishmen,' who have given part of their youth to fight Powers which used it. As for Razumov, his type has become familiar, though the set of circumstances in which it appears has altered, scarcely for the better. Conrad, throughout his narrative, retains a slightly contemptuous sympathy for him, that wretched man who, at the time of his worst apprehensions regarding Haldin, wrote in a neat, unsteady, almost child-like handwriting, five short phrases one under the other:

> History not Theory.
> Patriotism not Internationalism.
> Evolution not Revolution.
> Direction not Destruction.
> Unity not Disruption.

For Miss Haldin, as for so many of his heroines, Conrad shows unqualified admiration; for the group of revolutionaries, indeed for Russians as a whole, almost unrelieved contempt. What he most remarks is 'the Russians' extraordinary love of words. They gather them up; they cherish them; they are always ready to pour them out . . . with such an aptness of application sometimes that, as in the case of very accomplished parrots, one can't defend oneself from the suspicion that they really understand what they say.'

Both sides in this extraordinary country, he seems to infer, are plain wrong. The ruthless cruelty of the bureaucracy and the unrealistic vanity of the anarchists are equally futile. What would have disturbed and annoyed Conrad most was the verdict of some later critics that *Under Western Eyes* is in fact a Russian novel written in English, and thus without the attendant disadvantages of translation. The observation has some truth, if it be added that it is a Russian novel of the finest kind.

VICTORY (1915)

'The best genius,' wrote Goethe in his last letter to Von Humboldt, 'is that which absorbs and assimilates everything without doing the least violence to its fundamental destiny.' Heyst, the hero of *Victory*, would have agreed with him. Unfortunately for himself, he had early been uprooted, his outlook on life profoundly influenced by a disillusioned father, and although willing, almost eager, to do nothing more than to 'absorb,' he had been caught up by life, so that it was he himself who, unwillingly enough, had become part of the 'fundamental destiny' of others. Seldom in Conrad is the reader made so aware of the importance of chance in the affairs of an individual. In the case of Heyst he is whirled away, despite himself, into a series of events and situations in which he finds passivity impossible.

As a human being, Heyst is not Conrad's most convincing creation, though he once said that '*Victory* is a book in which I have tried to grasp at more life-stuff than perhaps in any other of my works.' Its power and beauty lie rather in its incidents, and in the contrast between the forces of good and evil, which are here set forth with bold strokes.

Heyst, says Conrad, had 'learned to reflect, which is a destructive process, a reckoning of the cost. It is not the clear-sighted who rule the world. Great achievements are accomplished in a blessed, warm mental fog.' Heyst's idea is that life should be 'a solitary achievement accomplished not by hermit-like withdrawal with its silence and immobility, but by a system of restless wandering, by the detachment of an impermanent dweller amongst changing scenes. In this scheme he had perceived the means of passing through life without suffering and almost without a single care in the world—invulnerable because elusive.' He had, in fact, discovered the world to be 'a factory, and all mankind workmen in it.' But 'the wages were not good enough,' and 'were paid in counterfeit money.'

Heyst is, twice at least, moved by sympathy to direct intervention in the lives of others. First he befriends Morrison, a ship's captain who appears to be cornered by fate. He saves him from ruin, only to be almost overwhelmed by gratitude, and to realize later that his action has been misinterpreted by those who do not know the facts. 'No decent feeling was ever scorned by Heyst.' That, not the bland or cynical detachment inherited from his father, is the true keynote of his character. The paternal attitude of life has indeed impressed him—but not enough.

Having escaped entanglement with the embarrassing Morrison, Heyst reaches a second, more acute stage of re-education. He finds, quite by chance, that a German restaurant keeper, Schomberg, whose establishment figures from time to time as part of Conrad's Malayan background, has amorous designs on a girl, Lena. She herself is almost as imperfectly realized, in terms of flesh and blood, as is Heyst himself. Lena is by circumstances at the mercy of a sinister character called Zangiacomos, who runs a travelling concert-party. Moved by a glimpse he is given of her wretched life, Heyst contrives to escape with her to an island—the novel's sub-title is 'An Island Tale'—which he had once intended as his private refuge. The incident of the escape, effected by means of Schomberg's unregarded wife right under the German's very nose, has a swiftness and tension which Conrad could summon, in his best years, almost at will.

It is not Lena herself who moves Heyst. Neither had it been Morrison. It is their fate. 'No decent feeling was ever scorned by Heyst'; and therein lies his destiny. He cannot free himself from the effects of his own impulses. As for Lena, 'he had no illusions about her, but his sceptical mind was dominated by his heart.'

As is its way, the outside world is not so appreciative of Heyst as Heyst himself is of the troubles of his fellows. He learns from Lena that Schomberg, who has from the first taken an obsessive dislike to him, has spread slander about him in the matter of Morrison. And now this same German, thirsting for revenge for the trick which has baulked him of Lena, sets the forces of evil in pursuit of the pair. Ricardo, a 'secretary,' who is described in plain terms as 'the embodied evil of the world,' descends upon the island with his equally odious master Jones, and an anthropoid follower Pedro, 'a spectre, a cat and an ape,' as even Schomberg calls them. Tragedy has become inevitable.

From the outset, the relationship between Lena and Heyst has been uneasy, almost unnatural. It remains so until towards the close of the book. Lena, woman-like, probes into the facts of Heyst's past relationship with Morrison, and it dawns upon her that her own situation is beginning to offer a parallel. Heyst, it becomes clear, wishes to save rather than to possess her. With her woman's logic, she also perceives that it was not, in the first place, affection for Morrison which led Heyst to help him. It was something else. She puts it clumsily, indeed in the stilted manner which informs much of the dialogue.

'You saved a man for fun—is that what you mean? Just for fun?'—she asks, and one feels that her questing must have had a touch of desperation.

'Why this tone of suspicion?' asks Heyst. 'I suppose the sight of this particular distress was disagreeable to me. What you call fun came afterwards, when it dawned on me that I was for him a walking, breathing, incarnate proof of the efficacy of prayer. I was a little fascinated by it—and then, could I have argued with him? You don't argue against such evidence, and besides, it would have looked as if I wanted to claim the merit. Already his gratitude was simply frightful. Funny position, wasn't it? The boredom came later, when we lived together on board his ship. I had, in a moment of inadvertence, created for myself a tie. How to define it precisely I don't know. One gets attached in a way to people one has done something for. But is that friendship? I am not sure what it was. I only know that he who forms a tie is lost.'

The later part of the story, when Jones, Pedro and Ricardo are on the island, is in part melodramatic. Conrad had shown this characteristic in his first books, *Almayer's Folly* and *An Outcast of the Islands*. Many years' practice had improved his powers of suspense, but these were always considerable. The final chapters of *Victory* for all their strained emphasis are of a sustained excitement unsurpassed, and not often equalled, in the novels. In one of the final scenes Lena, mortally wounded but having disarmed the most dangerous oppenent, dies 'convinced of the reality of her victory over death.' Her relation with Heyst, imperfect as it has been, has nerved her to deal with the forces of evil. 'She was no longer alone.'

The passage in which her death is described is a fine

one, and it is small wonder that it should have moved Conrad's American audience when he read it aloud. Lena has disobeyed Heyst in order to save him. She has gone to Ricardo, and Heyst, for a fleeting moment, thinks she may have betrayed him. 'No doubt you acted from instinct,' he says. 'Women have been provided with their own weapon. I was a disarmed man, I have been a disarmed man all my life as I see it now. You may glory in your resourcefulness and your profound knowledge of yourself; but I may say that the other attitude, suggestive of shame, had its charm, for you are full of charm.'

Lena, in fact, has been shot by Jones, who had intended his bullet for the secretary Ricardo, who has turned traitor. Heyst does not know this until Lena drops, her hand to her breast, her wound mortal:

' "Who else could have done this for you?" she whispered gloriously.

' "No one in the world," he answered her in a murmur of unconcealed despair.

'She tried to raise herself, but all she could do was to lift her head a little from the pillow. With a terrified and gentle movement, Heyst hastened to slip his arm under her neck. She felt relieved at once of an intolerable weight, and was content to surrender to him the infinite weariness of her tremendous achievement. Exulting, she saw herself extended on the bed, in a black dress, and profoundly at peace; while, stooping over her with a kindly playful smile, he was ready to lift her up in his firm arms and take her into the sanctuary of his innermost heart—for ever! The flush of rapture flooding her whole being broke out in a smile of innocent, girlish happiness; and with that divine radiance on her lips she breathed her last, triumphant, seeking for his glance in the shades of death.'

*   *   *

It is always easy, and tempting, to quote from Conrad, and nowhere are extracts more likely to lead to a false impression than when they are taken from *Victory*. The anthologists, with shrewdness, usually stick to his scenic passages, and his more showy observations on life in general. In his dialogue, it is Conrad's cumulative force which matters, his patient building up of character by means of talk which in isolated passages may sometimes seem unnatural.

The language of *Victory*—and this even extends to the Preface—is, too often, not merely stilted, but seems to belong to the novelette. Nevertheless, the book as a whole is charged with such intense feeling that imperfections are overlooked by the reader, unless the necessity for analysis overtakes him. It is meant to be accepted, and, beyond question, it succeeds. Few responsible critics fail to place it among his best books, and it is so despite its flaws in detail.

Victory does not add to Conrad's stature as a portrayer of humanity, but as a story its force and assurance are considerable, and it marks a distinct change in his general attitude to the world. For he here reaffirms what he had already made plain in a less fine novel, *Chance* (1913), his belief in disinterested action. It is a factor which many so-called realists have hesitated to admit. Conrad had not only met it, or so the reader feels, but it had seemed to him profoundly necessary to record it.

Victory stands a little apart from the rest of the Eastern series. It was not to be the last story set in the enchanted seas, but it is the finest. It is the most graceful part of that highly coloured pattern with which he had first delighted his audience.

THE ROVER (1923)

The Rover stands in relation to the rest of Conrad's work as *The Tempest* does to that of Shakespeare. In it, although he took a less deliberate farewell of the world, he showed all his old mastery of narrative, all his sureness in building up the physical appearance of people and places, and he wrote with a serenity seldom to be found in his earlier books. Everything is managed and controlled with precision. There is rarely a word too much, and it is perhaps the only one of his full-length novels which might have been written by a Frenchman: for there is a Gallic simplicity of idea and of sentence, and it is 'simple' in the best sense of the word.

Nothing further was published in his lifetime except the dramatic version of the grim story of the Verlocs, and, even had *Suspense* been finished, with Napoleon at last recorded in his pages, it is inconceivable—judging by the extant portion—that it could have been so good. If the goddess who presides over the destinies of writers denied him one cherished ambition, she at least saw to it that he ended his career with dignity. Although *The Rover* did not belong to his finest decade—the wonderful years which produced *Nostromo*, *The Mirror*, his two Revolutionary novels, *Chance*, *Victory* and more than one consummate story, as the novel of an Indian summer it could scarcely be improved upon.

Once again the idea of loneliness predominates. Jean Peyrol, master-gunner, and a seaman who has had a piratical past, brings his ship home to Toulon, where he pays her off. She is state-owned, and as he views her masters thronging the quaysides, the heirs of the French Revolution, he feels he has seldom beheld a sorrier set of people.

Peyrol, like the hero of Defoe's *Captain Singleton*, has achieved a feat rare enough in life to be the subject of a story. He has got away with his plunder. He carries it on his person, sewn in a sail-cloth coat. For more than one good reason, he leaves the port of Toulon as soon as possible. There is nothing officially recorded against him, nothing whatever: but he has entered a country where suspicion is in the air. The worst fumes of the Revolution are dispersed, but France is still at war, allegiances are shifty, and Peyrol's paramount intention is to end his days quietly.

A lonely man, though a vigorous, practical and determined one, he makes for a lonely countryside, which he had known as a child. Childhood and poverty had brought him few joys, but a homing instinct is upon him, and he finds something more than mere refuge in the farm of Escampobar. It is on the Giens peninsula, which divides the roadstead of Hèyres 'from the headlands and curves of the coast, forming the approaches of the port of Toulon.' It is a place of great beauty. Within it the whole main action of the story takes place. Conrad was careful, in *The Rover*, to observe those unities upon which Aristotle and all classical critics were insistent. They make the classical drama; and they add to the effect of even the feeblest romance.

The Escampobar household is a curious one. There is an elderly woman, Catherine, of much force of character, and a young girl, Arlette, who is the heroine of the story. Arlette's parents have been slaughtered in the Revolution. She herself, as a child, has beheld scenes of carnage such as would have unbalanced the staunchest adult. Her mind when the story opens is, as it were, dormant. Her physical survival is due to a strange, fanatical creature called Scevola Bron, who is the Caliban of the tale. He is one of the many who have been thrown up, and discarded, by the most violent forces of the time. He is execrable, but like Arlette, though in a more fundamental way, he is incomplete. In his fashion, he loves her.

In order to give himself an even securer attachment to a place to which he is attracted, Peyrol acquires the semi-derelict tartane which has brought Scevola and Arlette back from the Toulon of foul memory. He puts the craft in order; and in this he is helped by a local cripple, the fisherman Michel who, despite his physical drawbacks, is the best man in his native place. Giving a new life to this little vessel, fitting her out perfectly and concealing her with skill, gives Peyrol an increasingly vivid interest in his home-coming.

As France is at war, she is under close blockade from the English fleet. The main body lies out of sight, commanded by Nelson, 'wearing away the last two years of his glorious but suffering life, fighting the fierce north-westers of the Gulf of Lyons and questioning, questioning continually with feverish anxiety, whether Napoleon's object was Egypt or Great Britain. They were dull, weary, eventless months, these months of watching and waiting of the big ships before the French arsenals. Purposeless they surely seemed to many . . . but the world has never seen a more impressive demonstration of the influence of sea-power upon its history. Those far-distant, storm-beaten ships, upon which the Grand Army never looked, stood between it and the dominion of the world.'

The passage is from Mahan, and illustrates perfectly the importance of the events and the background of the time. Light vessels serve as the admiral's eyes, and one of them is upon that stretch of coast behind which lies Escampobar. Peyrol finds a constant if bitter pleasure in watching the seamanlike manœuvres of Captain Vincent of the English sloop *Amelia*.

There soon appears another important character, in the person of Lieutenant Réal. He is a regular naval officer, who at first views Peyrol with suspicion. He guesses what he has been, though, like his superiors, he has no proof. Peyrol is not perturbed. On first coming to Escampobar he had won over the wild Arlette, since 'he knew how to be patient, with that patience that is so often a form of courage. He was known for it. It had served him well in dangerous situations.' He will win Réal.

Arlette falls in love with Réal, and in a scene of wonderful vividness she goes to the church, which she has not before visited. She tells the abbé the dreadful details of her early days, and she is told to pray. She does so.

' "You have prayed well, my daughter," says the abbé. "No forgiveness will be refused to you, for you have suffered much. Put your trust in the grace of God."

'She raised her head and stayed her footsteps for a moment. In the dark little place he could see the gleam of her eyes swimming in tears.

' "Yes, Monsieur l'Abbé," she said in her clear seductive voice. "I have prayed and I feel answered. I entreated the merciful God to keep the heart of the man I love always true to me or else to let me die before I set eyes upon him again."

'The abbé paled under his tan of a village priest and leaned his shoulders against the wall without a word.'

K

How Arlette wins Réal's love, and how Peyrol in his
tartane deceives the English fleet as to the immediate
intention of the French, are the subjects of the later part
of the book. Peyrol leads the *Amelia* off her station in
such a convincing chase that the English captain becomes
certain she is concerned in an important mission. At last
he closes, and, as Peyrol refuses to heave the tartane to,
it is necessary to order the marines to fire. Peyrol is hit.
   'A feeling of peace sank into him, not unmingled
with pride. Everything he had planned had come to pass.
He had meant to play that man a trick, and now the
trick had been played. Played by him better than by any
other old man on whom age had stolen, unnoticed, till
the veil of peace was torn down by the touch of a sentiment unexpected like an intruder and cruel like an
enemy.' His last fear, before death, is that Captain
Vincent will run him down, 'and sink the despatches
together with the craft.' But everything succeeds perfectly; it always does with Peyrol. The English captain
who 'could not refuse his admiration' of the white-
haired man of the tartane, has an interview with Nelson.
   ' "You have a very smart little ship, Vincent," says
the Admiral, "very fit for the work I have given you to
do. French built, isn't she?"
   ' "Yes, my lord. They are great ship-builders."
   ' "You don't seem to hate the French, Vincent," said
the Admiral, smiling faintly.
   ' "Not that kind, my lord," said Captain Vincent with
a bow. . . .'
He leaves the Admiral, 'feeling, like all officers who
approached Lord Nelson, that he had been speaking with
a personal friend.' Conrad was robbed of his Napoleon,
and one is grateful for this slight brush with a man who
was in his differing way quite as illustrious.

The Rover ends happily. The tartane is sunk with her French ensign flying, and Réal, after he 'sailed away with the Toulon fleet on the great strategical cruise which was to end in the Battle of Trafalgar,' where he was wounded, later returns to marry his Arlette. They are haunted, but happily haunted, by the memory of old Peyrol.

The final sentences run: 'The blue level of the Mediterranean, the charmer and the deceiver of audacious men, kept the secret of its fascination—hugged to its calm breast the victims of all the wars, calamities and tempests of its history, under the marvellous purity of the sunset sky. A few rosy clouds floated high up over the Esterel range. The breath of the coming breeze came to cool the heated rocks of Escampobar; and the mulberry tree, the only big tree on the head of the peninsula, standing like a sentinel at the gate of the yard, sighed faintly in a shudder of all its leaves as if regretting the Brother of the Coast, the man of dark deeds, but of large heart, who often at noonday would lie down to sleep under its shade.'

*   *   *

The Rover raises one speculation which is not much furthered by *Suspense*. How would Conrad have succeeded with an historical series? In itself, it is as near flawless as it could be, but it is on a smaller scale than his other supreme novels. It grew from a story, like *Lord Jim*, and the action is played out by a very circumscribed group of characters. It does not tell us quite enough about the author's historical imagination; nor do, for instance, stories like 'The Duel' and 'The Inn of the Two Witches' which are also ventures into the past in the sense known to professed historical novelists.

Conrad had a shrewd sense of history, and perhaps the most that can be said is that, if the Napoleonic idea had been worked upon in his vigorous years instead of in his last, he would probably have written an historical novel comparable in its own genre with the splendid *Nostromo*. Such, at any rate, is the feeling given to at least one reader by the understanding shown in *The Rover*.

As it is, Conrad's greater novels include two which are concerned, primarily, with moral problems, *Lord Jim* and *Victory*; three which show a wider consideration of society, *Nostromo*, *The Secret Agent* and *Under Western Eyes*; and a valediction, in *The Rover*, which gives rise to a score of 'mights,' had other subjects than history not pressed themselves upon him in his earlier days.

To have written one great novel has been the ardent wish of many who have devoted themselves with single-ness of purpose. In the light of that aspiration, Conrad may indeed seem to have carried, like his own Peyrol, a coat of gold.

GREATER STORIES

I T is certainly true that Conrad is better known by his stories than his novels. This may be odd, but it is unlikely to change. When Virginia Woolf wrote her tribute, soon after the news of his death, she said: 'Though we shall make expeditions into the later books and bring back wonderful trophies, large tracts of them will remain by most of us untrodden. It is the earlier books—*Youth*, *Lord Jim*, *Typhoon*, *The Nigger of the 'Narcissus'* that we shall read in their entirety.' Her prophecy, up to this time, has not proved far wrong, and it is therefore fortunate that in his longer stories Conrad was so often excellent. Of her four examples, only *Lord Jim* is full-length, and there is the old complaint—that it is more of an elongated 'tale' than a conventional novel.

It is not length alone, which is of itself unimportant, that distinguishes many of the stories from the major novels. They possess one special quality, in that, with a few exceptions, they are closely autobiographical. Conrad had some aptitude for invention; but in such stories as *The Nigger*, 'Youth,' 'Typhoon' and 'Heart of Darkness' the quality was not required. His need was merely to remember, and so to reassemble his material that it had the artistic shape so often lacking in day-to-day life. For the difference between art and life may surely be expressed as the gulf which lies between the phrases 'It so happened' and '*It happened so.*'

THE NIGGER OF THE 'NARCISSUS' (1897)

Conrad regarded *The Nigger of the 'Narcissus'* as one of the works by which he would like to have been judged, the 'decent edifice' he wished to put up in honour of the men with whom he had lived in the forecastle. 'They had been strong,' he says of them, 'as he is strong who neither doubts nor hopes. They had been impatient and enduring, turbulent and deserted, unruly and faithful. . . . Men hard to manage, but easy to inspire: voiceless men—but men enough to scorn in their hearts the sentimental voices that bewailed the hardness of their fate.'

Conrad knew life before the mast with the familiarity only given to those who have spent their most impressionable years risking limb to earn a meagre wage, observing the sea in all her moods, dependent upon their own skill for safety. So *The Nigger*, for all its elaborate motif of Wait's strange illness, the trouble his sickness causes, the speculation as to whether it is genuine, and his death at sea which seems to give immediate relief to the ship and to her men, is simply an account of a stormy voyage which reproduces the very accents and murmurs of the forecastle hands. They are tried to desperation: they verge upon mutiny, but there is never serious doubt that Captain Allistoun, a man who is packed with resource in face of bad weather, will deal readily enough with mere human insubordination.

Neither the master nor the nigger are, in a sense, paramount figures. It is the *Narcissus* herself and her seamen who are at once the subjects and the heroes of the story. This, the reader feels, is the true life of the sailor of old time, the life at which we have to guess when we see the spick husk of the *Victory*. It has no glamour, but it is not without heroism. Reading of it, one may savour the humour in Dr. Johnson's sentence that 'No man will be a sailor who has contrivance enough to get himself into a gaol; for being in a ship is being in a gaol, with the chance of being drowned.'

There are, of course, compensations, moments of sheer beauty, felt even by the weary men: as when the *Narcissus* enters the chops of the Channel. 'Under white wings she skimmed low over the blue sea like a great tired bird speeding to its nest. The clouds raced with her mast-heads; they rose astern enormous and white, soared to the zenith, flew past, and, falling down the white curve of the sky, seemed to dash headlong into the sea—the clouds swifter than the ship, more free, but without a home. The coast to welcome her stepped out of space into the sunshine. The lofty headlands trod masterfully into the sea; the wide bays smiled in the light; the shadows of homeless clouds ran along the sunny plains, leaped over valleys, without a check darted up the hills, rolled down the slopes; and the sunshine pursued them with patches of running brightness. . . . The *Narcissus* rushed past the headlands and the bays. Outward-bound vessels crossed her track, lying over, with their masts stripped for a slogging fight with a hard sou'wester. And inshore, a string of smoking steamboats waddled, hugging the coast, like migrating and amphibious monsters, distrustful of the restless waves.'

Conrad's own note upon *The Nigger*, part of which has been quoted in the Preface to this book, is important in that it expresses concisely his artistic creed in general, and his intention in this particular story. His immediate purpose is 'to arrest, for the space of a breath, the hands busy about the work of the earth, and compel men entranced by the sight of distant goals to glance for a moment at the surrounding vision of form and colour, of sunshine and shadows; to make them pause for a look, for a sigh, for a smile—such is the aim, difficult and evanescent, and reserved only for a very few to achieve. But sometimes, by the deserving and the fortunate, even that task is accomplished, and when it is accomplished —behold! all the truth of life is there: a moment of vision, a sigh, a smile—and the return to an eternal rest.'

The Nigger is in some ways a landmark. It was Conrad's first excursion into a realm he was to develop with infinite variation. Although by no means the best of his longer stories, it was, for him, a 'necessary' book. It was one, he told Garnett (to whom it is dedicated), that he felt he owed to his friends. Having achieved it he had given himself the freedom to draw more particular portraits, to become at once more personal and more philosophical. *The Nigger* is a conversation piece on a memorable scale, a portrayal of a set of men the like of whom had made his adopted country great. Not only was it his first long-short-story of calibre; it would be some years before he would write a successor fit to compare with it. When at last he did so, it appeared in a volume which, even by itself, should have secured the reputation of any writer.

YOUTH[1]

The volume called *Youth* contains three long stories, the title-story, 'Heart of Darkness,' and 'The End of the Tether.' Each of them shows Conrad majestic. He once said, in a letter, that their juxtaposition was

[1] *Youth* (1902).

deliberate, his intention being to represent three ages in man: youth, maturity and age, though he made a prefatory remark that the stories 'lay no claim to unity of artistic purpose.'

'Youth' was pure memory. Conrad related what had happened to him in the barque *Palestine*, which, coal-laden and leaky, had caught fire and been destroyed in the tropics on her way to Bangkok. It was written quickly, at the invitation of Mr. William Blackwood for 'Maga,' with whose readers it was a great success. Conrad could have told the story directly, had he so wished; but in it he introduced his narrator, Marlow, for the first time. 'Of all my people,' he said, 'he's the one that has never been a vexation to my spirit. A most discreet, understanding man'; in fact, the 'Maga' personality.

Apart from the change in the name of the vessel from *Palestine* to *Judea* (or *'Judea*. London, *Do or Die'*—as Conrad described the legend on her stern) the title-story is well related fact, and there is not much more to be said about it than that. Some of the prose is purple enough; 'Q,' for instance, could not resist it for *The Oxford Book of English Prose*, and it is valuable as expressing Conrad's first feelings about the East and its people.

The narrator comes upon them after the ship has burnt out, and after he, with his boat-load of castaways, has reached safety at the cost of utter exhaustion. 'And then I saw the men of the East,' he says: '. . . I saw brown, bronze, yellow faces, the black eyes, the glitter, the colour of an Eastern crowd. And all these beings stared without a murmur, without a sigh, without a movement. They stared down at the boats, at the sleeping men who at night had come to them from the sea.

Nothing moved. The fronds of the palms stood still against the sky. Not a branch stirred along the shore, and the brown roofs of hidden houses peeped through the green foliage, through the big leaves that hung shining and still like leaves forged of heavy metal. This was the East of the ancient navigators, so old, so mysterious, resplendent and sombre, living and unchanged, full of danger and promise.'

The passage continues, romantically, until the well-known sentence: 'Tell me, wasn't that the best time, that time when we were young at sea; young and had nothing, on the sea that gives nothing, except hard knocks—and sometimes a chance to feel your strength . . . ?' and the final phrases: 'our weary eyes looking still, looking always, looking anxiously for something out of life, that while it is expected is already gone—has passed unseen, in a sigh, in a flash—together with the youth, with the strength, with the romance of illusions.'

HEART OF DARKNESS[1]

By quoting a significant sentence from 'Heart of Darkness' as an epigraph for *The Hollow Men* ('Mistah Kurtz, he dead') Mr. T. S. Eliot will have sent more than one reader to the original. They can have felt no disappointment, since it is one of Conrad's finest things. It is 'experience pushed a little (and only very little) beyond the actual facts of the case.' It relates the story of a journey up the Congo in a river steamer. One of the purposes of this voyage is to relieve Kurtz, an agent of the company to whom the steamer belongs. They find Kurtz living in a scene of 'incredible' horror— Conrad worked his adjectives hard in this story—far

[1] *Youth* (1902).

inside the darkness of an evil land. When they reach their destination, and Marlow's eyes fall on Kurtz's living-place, he sees through his glasses a mysterious line of posts.

'You remember,' he says, 'I had been struck at the distance by certain attempts at ornamentation, rather remarkable in the ruinous aspect of the place. Now I had suddenly a nearer view, and its first result was to make me throw my head back as if before a blow. Then I went carefully from post to post with my glass, and I saw my mistake. Those round knobs were not ornamental but symbolic; they were expressive and puzzling, striking and disturbing—food for thought and also for the vultures if there had been any looking down from the sky; but at all events for such ants as were industrious enough to ascend the pole. They would have been even more impressive, those heads on stakes, if their faces had not been turned to the house. Only one, the first I had made out, was facing my way. I was not so shocked as you may think. The start back I had given was really nothing but a movement of surprise. I had expected to see a knob of wood there, you know. I returned deliberately to the first I had seen—and there it was, black, dried, sunken, with closed eyelids—a head that seemed to sleep at the top of that pole, and, with the shrunken dry lips showing a narrow white line of the teeth, was smiling too, smiling continuously at some endless and jocose dream of that eternal slumber.

'I am not disclosing any trade secrets. In fact, the manager said afterwards that Mr. Kurtz's methods had ruined the district. I have no opinion on that point, but I want you clearly to understand that there was nothing exactly profitable in those heads being there. They only showed that Mr. Kurtz lacked restraint in the gratification of his various lusts, that there was some-thing wanting in him—some small matter which, when the pressing need arose, could not be found under his magnificent eloquence. Whether he knew of this defi-ciency himself I can't say. I think the knowledge came to him at last—only at the very last, but the wilderness had found him out early, and had taken on him a terrible vengeance for the fantastic invasion. I think it had whispered to him things about himself which he did not know, things of which he had no conception till he took counsel with this great solitude—and the whisper had proved irresistibly fascinating. It echoed loudly within him because he was hollow at the core. . . .'

Kurtz has not merely thrown off civilization, he resents it fiercely, and is unwilling to return. He is desperately ill, and in fact dies on the steamer during the return journey.

'He cried in a whisper at some image, at some vision —he cried out twice, a cry that was no more than a breath—

' "The horror! The horror!"

'I blew the candle out and left the cabin. The pil-grims were dining in the mess-room, and I took my place opposite the manager, who lifted his eyes to give me a questioning glance, which I successfully ignored. He leaned back, serene, with that peculiar smile of his sealing the unexpressed depth of his meanness. A con-tinuous shower of small flies streamed upon the lamp, upon the cloth, upon our hands and faces. Suddenly the manager's boy put his insolent face in the doorway, and said in a tone of scathing contempt—

' "Mistah Kurtz—he dead."

'All the pilgrims rushed out to see. I remained, and went on with my dinner. I believe I was considered brutally callous. However, I did not eat much. There was a lamp in there—light, don't you know—and outside it was so beastly, beastly dark.'

When Marlow at last returns to Europe, after an experience which marked him for the rest of his life, one of his duties is to break the news of Kurtz's death to the woman who loves him. She is an idealist, one of those creatures who appear in Conrad's pages not so much as women of reality as visions setting off men or circumstances.

'"You were with him—to the last?"' she says, in accents which, the reader feels, insist on a romantic picture. "I think of his loneliness. Nobody near to understand him as I would have understood. Perhaps no one to hear. . . ."

'"To the very end," I said shakily. "I heard his very last words . . ." I stopped in a fright.

'"Repeat them," she murmured in a heartbroken tone. '"I want—I want—something—something to live with."

'I was on the point of crying at her, "Don't you hear them?" The dark was repeating them in a persistent whisper all around us, in a whisper that seemed to swell menacingly, like the first whisper of a rising wind. "The horror! The horror!"

'"His last words—to live with," she insisted. "Don't you understand I loved him—I loved him—I loved him!"

'I pulled myself together and spoke slowly.

'"The last word he pronounced was—your name."

'I heard a light sigh and then my heart stood still, stopped dead short by an exulting and terrible cry, by the cry of inconceivable triumph and of unspeakable pain.

'"I knew it—I was sure!" . . . She knew. She was sure.'

*   *   *

Conrad's irony was never more pointed than in
'Heart of Darkness.' His loathing of the Congo, of the
whole Central African scene, drove him to some of his
best writing. Even before Marlow reaches the Congo,
there are memorable pictures, such as when the ship
passes a gunboat 'dropping shells into Africa.'

'There wasn't even a shed there, and she was shelling
the bush. It appears the French had one of their wars
going on thereabouts. Her ensign dropped limp like a
rag; the muzzles of the long six-inch guns stuck out all
over the low hull; the greasy, slimy swell swung her up
lazily and let her down, swaying her thin masts. In the
empty immensity of earth, sky and water, there she was,
incomprehensible, firing into a continent. Pop, would
go one of the six-inch guns; a small flame would dart and
vanish, a tiny projectile would give a feeble screech—
and nothing happened. Nothing could happen. There
was a touch of insanity in the proceeding, a sense of
lugubrious drollery in the sight; and it was not dissipated
by somebody on board assuring me earnestly there was
a camp of natives—he called them enemies!—hidden out
of sight somewhere.'

'A touch of insanity in the proceeding': it is, indeed,
at the core of 'Heart of Darkness' though it is never the
madness of inconsequence. The writing of it, and of the
earlier, equally horrific Congo story *An Outpost of
Progress* would have afforded Conrad infinite relief. Both
are overladen stories. They carry a greater emotional
charge than is quite consistent with their form: but this
is rare and excusable.

THE END OF THE TETHER[1]

'The End of the Tether' differs markedly from its companions in scene, in mood, in manner. By comparison it is quiet and objective. Captain Whalley is one of Conrad's noble portraits, and his story is simple. He is a man whom time rather than the world has used hardly, a fine old seaman reduced by circumstances to partnership in an eastern steamer with an engineer officer who is not merely contemptible but eccentric in a dangerous sense. Most tragic fact of all, Whalley is losing his sight. He is, in fact, only kept going because he knows his route beyond reasonable possibility of mistake, and because of his complete reliance on his faithful Malay quartermaster. Why he wishes to continue at all is due to love for his daughter in Australia, who needs all the help he can give her in her struggle with poverty. She supports an invalid husband, and has difficulty in making ends meet by means of a boarding-house.

Whalley is betrayed by his partner, who covets the insurance on his rotten vessel. A coat, loaded with iron, is placed near the binnacle to falsify the compass. The ship runs in the night upon a rocky ledge, and, 'in that old heart, in that vigorous body there was, that nothing should be wanting, a horror of death that apparently could not be overcome by the horror of blindness.' Nevertheless, Whalley goes down with the *Sofala* into the darkness, the only man lost, the only man who would never lie about the cause of the disaster.

No flaw marks Whalley's character or intentions. Conrad portrayed many good men, but none who appeal more directly to the heart, or who are more complete

[1] *Youth* (1902).

in their reality. It is good to know, from Mr. Curle, that 'of all his male characters Conrad had most affection for Captain Whalley.'

'Life,' he says, through the thoughts which flow through the mind of Whalley's daughter when she learns of the tragedy, 'life had been too hard, for all the efforts of his love. It had silenced her emotions. . . . Gone! Was it possible? The blow had come softened by the spaces of the earth, by the years of absence. There had been whole days when she had not thought of him at all —had no time. But she had loved him, she felt she had loved him after all.'

In no other story does Conrad make the reader so aware of the unimportance of mere propinquity. Life may press heavily, so heavily at times as to squeeze memory aside: but what is permanent in human relationships remains so in spite of everything. It is the idea that matters; nothing else is comparable with it.

TYPHOON[1]

The true companion-piece to *The Nigger*, the one other story in which a great storm figures, is 'Typhoon.' It followed closely upon 'The End of the Tether' and is notable chiefly for the character of Captain MacWhirr, the man who, in his small steamer, defeats the worst the elements can offer. It has a touch of the grotesque: the *Nan-Shan* is full of wretched Chinamen flung about down below, their private stores of silver dollars inextricably mingled; and even the storm itself takes on an almost eccentric violence. Typhoons are, so those who have survived them say, utterly monstrous in their force. Since Conrad's time at least one other mighty storm has blown

[1] *Typhoon and Other Stories* (1903).

through English fiction, in the pages of Mr. Richard Hughes's *In Hazard*. The process is that a ship, having survived the first assault, reaches comparative calm near the centre of the convulsion, and is then faced with the second and often the worse part of her ordeal. Conrad evaded the double trial. MacWhirr's buffeting in the early part of the story is severe enough, and is described in splendid detail: the final triumph is shown only by implication.

Perhaps it is enough; at any rate, MacWhirr has proved his metal. 'Don't you be put out by anything,' he says to one of his officers. 'Keep her facing it. They may say what they like, but the heaviest seas run with the wind. Facing it—always facing it!—that's the way to get through.' The words have their effect. Jukes, the officer spoken to, 'experienced an access of confidence, a sensation that came from outside like a warm breath, and made him feel equal to every demand. The distant muttering of the darkness stole into his ears. He noted it unmoved, out of that sudden belief in himself, as a man safe in a shirt of mail would watch a point.'

'Typhoon' is famous as a success-story—that of a man who, having got the better of the wind, was fully equal to solving, with rough justice, the human problem of the Chinamen and their dollars—and indeed anything else that came his way. The events are narrated largely by means of dialogue and by 'letters home' in which the understatement is terrific. It is one of Conrad's happier stories, renowned perhaps beyond its deserts, but none the less an inescapable sea-piece for all who would know the British sea-officer at his best.

Conrad could never resist irony. Here it is sportive. The *Nan-Shan* flies the flag of Siam. 'Fancy having a

L

ridiculous Noah's Ark elephant in the ensign of one's ship,' thinks Jukes. As for the captain, his almost Dickensian appearance is again not without comedy, in contrast with his actions at sea. 'He was rather below medium height,' says Conrad, 'a bit round-shouldered, and so sturdy of limb that his clothes always looked a shade too tight for his arms and legs. As if unable to grasp what is due to the difference of latitudes, he wore a brown bowler hat, a complete suit of a brownish hue, and clumsy black boots. These harbour togs gave to his thick figure an air of stiff and uncouth smartness. A thin silver watch-chain looped his waistcoat, and he never left his ship for the shore without clutching in his powerful, hairy fist an elegant umbrella of the very best quality, but generally unrolled. Young Jukes, the chief mate, attending his commander to the gangway, would sometimes venture to say, with the greatest gentleness, "Allow me, sir"—and, possessing himself of the umbrella deferentially, would elevate the ferrule, shake the folds, twirl a neat furl in a jiffy, and hand it back: going through the performance with a face of such portentous gravity that Mr. Solomon Rout, the chief engineer, smoking his morning cigar over the skylight, would turn away his head in order to hide a smile.

' "Oh! aye! The blessed gamp. . . . Thank'ee, Jukes, thank'ee," would mutter Captain MacWhirr heartily, without looking up.'

There is not a more affectionate cameo in Conrad's pages; and its general truth to life will be recognized by all who know the merchant marine.

As with *The Nigger*, there is nothing forced about 'Typhoon.' The *Nan-Shan* is not a special but a typical ship. Her triumphant emergence from trial is shown to be the natural result of traditions and methods of seafaring in which the word defeat is not merely un-mentioned, but unconsidered.

FALK[1]

The volume of stories in which 'Typhoon' appears also contains two other long stories, 'Amy Foster' and 'Falk,' together with a slighter piece, 'Tomorrow.' 'Amy Foster' is interesting as showing the effect of England and her people upon a poor Baltic seafarer cast away upon her shores. Even his wife, Amy Foster, who marries him partly from pity, cannot do more than grope in her understanding of him, and tragedy is inevitable from the first. It is of interest rather as a parable than as a story, and, as it corresponds closely with a tele-scoped version of some of the outward events of Conrad's own life, it has a certain flavour not to be found else-where. But for an example of his art as a story-teller, 'Falk' is outstanding in this particular collection.

'Falk's' background is almost that in which Conrad found his own *Otago*. In it, a ship is apparently doomed to stay in sheltered water, unable to put to sea due to the jealousy between Falk, a man of Olympian cast, the owner of the only tug in the river, and Hermann, a man whom he unreasonably fears. Hermann's niece, whom Falk loves, is as comely as he is: 'she could have stood for an allegoric statue of the Earth.'

But Falk is crippled by a memory of how, years before, he had saved his own life by murder, and main-tained it by cannibalism on a drifting vessel in the Southern Ocean. 'He was hungry for that girl,' says the narrator, 'terribly hungry, as he had once been hungry for food.' The romance, which is happily

[1] *Typhoon and Other Stories* (1903).

resolved, has a primitive vitality in keeping with its characters, and the picture of the Hermann family and their 'patriarchal old tub' has the clarity and colour of a painting by Van de Velde.

THE SECRET SHARER[1]

Conrad's collection, *A Set of Six*, which appeared in 1908, contained only one story, 'The Duel,' with a background of French military life, worthy to be considered representative; but in *'Twixt Land and Sea* (1912) he published two stories of high rank. 'A Smile of Fortune,' the story of a fortunate cargo, relates to the *Otago* days, and so, to a more vivid degree, does 'The Secret Sharer.'

In this tale, the narrator has just assumed his first command. His qualities are untried in the eyes of his ship's company, and he is scarcely aboard before he is visited by a refugee from justice. His name is Leggatt. This man swims alongside at dead of night and is given shelter.

Leggatt, a ship's officer, has taken life, in justifiable circumstances, during a storm at sea. He is 'a fugitive and a vagabond on the earth, with no brand of the curse on his sane forehead to stay a slaying hand.'

The young master, hearing his story, feels, as any man might: 'There, but for the Grace of God, go I.' He hides him, and the means of his concealment from the eyes of the steward and the ship's officers entails a mounting excitement which at times becomes almost unbearable. The ship is ordered to steer a dangerous course among the islands of the Gulf of Siam, for the master intends to drop Leggatt as close inshore as

[1] *'Twixt Land and Sea* (1912).

possible, so that he may swim away with a chance of safety.

'The black southern hill of Koh-Ting seemed to hang right over the ship like a towering fragment of the ever-lasting night,' runs a key passage. 'Then stillness again, with the great shadow gliding closer, towering higher, without light, without sound. Such a hush had fallen on the ship that she might have been a bark of the dead floating in slowly under the very gate of Erebus.'

The crew think the course a mad impulse of a mad young captain, but Leggatt escapes, the manœuvre suc-ceeds, and the ship is relieved of the Secret Sharer. Leggatt is, in fact, the captain's double, the man he might have been but for a happier twist of fortune. When Leggatt drops away into the darkness, the incident is not closed—it is merely suspended. We shall never hear what happened afterwards to Leggatt, but the lesson to be learnt from him may, we feel, be remem-bered as long as life.

FREYA OF THE SEVEN ISLES[1]

There is a third story in *'Twixt Land and Sea*, 'Freya of the Seven Isles,' which is one of the most pleasantly titled of Conrad's works. Yet it carries the note of tragedy almost from the first: the author does not even trouble to spare his reader foreknowledge of calamity, and in that sense it lacks surprise.

Freya, daughter of a Malayan trader, is loved by a man whose life, apart from her, is centred upon his ship. In this, the pair plan to live. The vessel is at once his livelihood and his pride. Freya is desired by Heemskirk, a Dutch naval officer who is one of the most unrelievedly

[1] *'Twixt Land and Sea* (1912).

brutal people in the whole Malayan series. He is gross both without and within, and he is not merely rejected by Freya; she laughs at his humiliation. So does her lover. A man such as Heemskirk could forgive little, ridicule least of all.

He has his full revenge, for by virtue of his position he can stop and search the ship at sea. This he does, and he then takes her in tow, ostensibly for detailed examination at the nearest Dutch port. Next, by a deft piece of seamanship, he runs her on a reef, and with her destroys for ever the happiness of the young couple.

There is no compensation for the gloom of the picture, no hint that justice will triumph even in the long run; nothing to indicate that Heemskirk ever feels a shadow of remorse. Conrad in fact offers nothing in this story but marvellous telling and, although it abounds in beauty and pity, 'Freya' affords no moral, no consolation, no wisdom except the bitter banality—do not make a fool of a Dutchman. Nevertheless, in so far as emotion can charge a story with vitality, 'Freya' is alive indeed.

*   *   *

Conrad's next collection, *Within the Tides* (1915), falls much short of his best. It is notable for a half-humorous sentence in the dedication, which speaks of 'this sheaf of care-free ante-bellum pages.' Actually there are four tales, each of which treats of violent death. By far the best is 'The Inn of the Two Witches,' a little gem in an historical setting, concerning the adventures of a sailor, landed during the Peninsular War, at an inn where he finds the body of a murdered shipmate.

But even 'The Inn of the Two Witches' is a slight matter by comparison with the greater stories of Conrad's best years, and there was, in fact, only one considerable piece of work to come. This was *The Shadow Line*.

THE SHADOW LINE (1917)

The Shadow Line, as Conrad says, 'belongs to that part of the Eastern Seas from which I have carried away into my writing life the greatest number of suggestions. It might have been called "First Command," for it is a reminiscence, personal experience seen in perspective with the eye of the mind and coloured by that affection one can't help feeling for such events of one's life as one has no reason to be ashamed of.' It is the story of the *Otago's* first voyage, haunted as she seemed by the ghost of her dead captain, and so riddled with sickness that her master and the cook, who though suffering from a weak heart is the only other fit seaman aboard, have to take her down the Gulf of Siam almost without help.

Although the voyage does indeed seem haunted, Conrad specifically disclaims the supernatural. 'I could never have attempted such a thing,' he says, 'because all my moral and intellectual being is penetrated by an invincible conviction that whatever falls under the domination of our senses must be of its nature, and, however exceptional, cannot differ in its essence from all the other effects of the visible and tangible world of which we are a self-conscious part. The world of the living contains enough marvels and mysteries as it is. . . .'

The Shadow Line is a sombre, solemn story with a triumphant conclusion, since the ship at last emerges from her trials. It is dedicated to Conrad's elder son Borys, at that time on the western front, and 'to all others who like himself have crossed in early youth the shadow-line of their generation.'

It is told in the first person, and Dr. Leavis, who actually ranks it higher than 'Heart of Darkness,' rightly calls it 'a supremely sinister and beautiful evocation of enchantment in tropic seas.' It is told directly, by the ship's master, that same man who, when they reach their destination, greets the naval surgeons who come to attend his men and the blue-jackets who furl his sails— 'a solitary figure in a blue and grey striped sleeping suit and a pipe-clayed helmet on its head.' Above all, it is notable for the portrait of Ransome the cook, who, having from professional pride, and at much cost in pain, helped the master to cross the shadow-line of trial, instantly demands his discharge. He has paid too high a price for his service to the ship, and, as he says, he 'has a right.' 'He gasped,' says Conrad, 'and a look of almost savage determination passed over his face. For an instant he was another being. And I saw under the worth and the comeliness of the man the humble reality of things. Life was a boon to him—this precarious, hard life—and he was thoroughly alarmed about himself.'

The story, fittingly, ends with Ransome. The master approaches him 'with extended hand. His eyes, not looking at me, had a strained expression. He was like a man listening for a warning call. "Won't you shake hands, Ransome?" I said gently. He exclaimed, flushed up dusky red, gave my hand a hard wrench—and next moment, left alone in the cabin, I listened to him going up the companion stairs cautiously, step by step, in mortal fear of starting into sudden anger our common enemy it was his hard fate to carry consciously within his faithful breast.'

*   *   *

There is no remaining story fit to compare with what

had gone before. In Conrad's posthumous collection, *Tales of Hearsay* (1925), there are few passages approaching his best, although it contains his one Polish story 'Prince Roman,' and his experimental, 'The Black Mate.'

'Prince Roman' is a portrait rather than a tale, and it was actually intended for a later book of reminiscences. It includes a moving evocation of the country to which the Prince has dedicated his sad life, that Poland 'which demands to be loved as no other country has ever been loved, with the mournful affection one bears to the unforgotten dead, and with the inextinguishable fire of a hopeless passion which only a living, breathing, warm ideal can kindle in our breasts, for our pride, for our weariness, for our exultation.'

If 'Prince Roman' is a straight portrait, and other stories are the purest autobiography, many of Conrad's lesser tales are no more than good craftsmanship. He never descended to trash, of which he would have been incapable, but he had to live, and it was natural, therefore, that not all his material should have been fully worthy of him. But in his shorter work the good so far outweighs the less good, is so easily separable from it, its extent is in some so considerable, that he must take rank as one of the most individual story writers who have used the English language. His best includes 'Heart of Darkness,' 'The End of the Tether,' 'The Secret Sharer,' 'The Shadow Line,' and a handful more.

He did not rank story-telling as a minor art, at any rate as regards difficulty, but he wrote his tales with proportionately greater ease than his novels: 'Youth' and 'Heart of Darkness,' which were written swiftly, are cases in point. It is certain that they gain from spontaneity, for Conrad was not always at his happiest when, as in his novel *Chance*, he forced complexity of plot as far as skill would allow. The simpler his manner, the surer his effect; it is almost a rule.

Conrad's expressed aim, in 'Heart of Darkness,' had been to give 'a sinister resonance, a tonality of its own, a continued vibration that, I hoped, would dwell on the ear after the last note had been struck.' He succeeded not there alone, but in those few stories by which he would himself have wished to be judged.

LESSER NOVELS

Five novels remain to be considered. They are *Almayer's Folly*, *An Outcast of the Islands*, *Chance*, *The Arrow of Gold* and *The Rescue*. Of them, only *Chance* might seem to call for extensive comment, since it is the one which has been held by certain thoughtful critics to rank with Conrad's best work. In fact, each of the five books has points of interest, and if they vary much in merit, *The Arrow of Gold* alone can be held scarcely worthy of the author's genius.

ALMAYER'S FOLLY (1895)

It is a well-observed truth that a first novel, if it have value, will possess it in one of two ways. Either it will be the author's only essential book, perhaps a good one, possibly—as with *Wuthering Heights*—supreme, but certainly carrying the mind's quintessence; or it will be prentice work, chiefly valuable as showing possibilities of future development—'a work of promise' in the well-worn phrase. It is the second type which makes the task of a publisher's reader one of difficulty, for it is his business to perceive what is sometimes only the thinnest vein of gold in a mass of rock. He must be more than patient; he must speculate, but prepare to find himself as disappointed as any other gambler.

One of the interests of *Almayer's Folly* is that it would have seemed good enough to go into the first category. By no possible means a *Wuthering Heights*, it is none the less a novel deserving serious attention on its own merits. It would have been worth publishing irrespective of anything the future might hold for the author. Yet in fact it belongs to the category of 'works of promise.'

M. Jean-Aubry calls Almayer a vivid example of that 'discord between the imagination in man and his power to perform, which was to be one dominant theme, at once magnificent and pathetic, of Conrad's work as an artist.' The remark is just, with the qualification that it is always the concrete instance that appeals to Conrad. 'I don't start with an abstract notion,' he wrote to Cunninghame Graham, 'I start with definite images, and as their rendering is true, some little effect is produced.'

His image of Almayer derived from a man he had met in Malaya, who had attracted him as a memorable, half-buried ruin might an archaeologist. Characteristic of Conrad's dark view of life was that he began with Almayer's final years, and harked back, in his second novel, to what he had once been.

Almayer's Folly is indeed a picture of decay. The story is that of a man who has been long settled in a trading post by an Eastern river. He has seen his friends, his marriage, his hopes and at last his trade disintegrate. Only one feeling keeps him sentient: it is love for his half-caste daughter, Nina. He has tried to educate her well, according to Western ideas. He hopes that she will prefer his own brand of civilization to that of her mother. But natural impulses are too strong for her, and Nina betrays his expectations in her love for a local chief, Dian. She breaks his heart. The story would be wholly tragic but for the happiness which Nina and Dian find in one another.

It was not the plot which struck Conrad's early readers. It was his power to evoke a scene. His characters are, by comparison with this, almost shadowy. The most vital human atmosphere belongs to Tom Lingard, a bold buccaneer to whom Almayer has owed his start. He appears and reappears, either in person or as a memory, in other Malayan tales, but his essential part in *Almayer* is that he haunts Almayer as a man who has shown success to be possible even in the enchanted but debilitating Archipelago.

Almayer, in its conjuring up of exotic scenes, contains passages of rich prose. These are what first attract attention, heightened later by the author's enthralled interest in racial differences, in the processes of despair, and in ironic twists of circumstance. Those who admired it demanded more of the same kind. It had struck a new note in fiction, and it was one which was to be continued by Conrad, intermittently, over many years.

AN OUTCAST OF THE ISLANDS (1896)

Almayer, if not answering to the idea of a hero, is drawn with understanding and tolerance. In *An Outcast of the Islands* Conrad took a shabby villain, Willems, as his centre of interest. Little redeems Willems. He has been a confidential clerk in a merchant house, and believes himself both clever and invaluable. His is not an uncommon type, and it is not pleasing. Actually Willems, far from being, as he supposes, on the way to fortune, has been tricked into marrying a Sirani girl who is his employer's natural daughter.

Willems embezzles, is found out, and in his turn betrays the secret entrance to the mouth of a trading river to a party of sea-Arabs. It is the key to country which Lingard and Almayer hope to exploit. Willems is, in fact, the agent of Almayer's later ruin, for when once the Arabs have come, the white men have no further prospect of riches. What is valuable will be taken by the intruders.

Willems and Almayer are at best uneasy neighbours. Willems is presently enmeshed in a passionate affair with a lovely native, Aissa, who is one of Conrad's more convincing women. Their affair has the heavy, demoralizing beauty of the background against which it unfolds.

As with *Victory*, the later part of the story is melodramatic, for Willems's Sirani wife reaches his sanctuary with her small child, and confronts him at the height of his affair with Aissa, who shoots her lover.

An Outcast, though it has more excitement, is on the whole a less interesting book than *Almayer*, since it is not so much a retrogression as a marking of time. It adds little to the already elaborate portrait of Almayer, and although Lingard as he here appears in the flesh has burly vigour, there is not much in *An Outcast* to show (what was in fact the case) that with Conrad's next venture, *The Nigger of the 'Narcissus,'* he would be at the gateway of his true kingdom. Once there, he would progress from one kind of triumph to another.

Seventeen years, and infinite development as an artist, separates *An Outcast* from *Chance*. They have scarcely a point in common, and it is merely for the reason that *Chance* seems a little less good than his best that it is included in this survey. Judged by any other standard, it is indeed a formidable novel.

CHANCE (1914)

Chance is Jamesian, utterly in the tradition of the Master. 'The politeness of Conrad to James and James to Conrad was of the most impressive kind,' says Ford

Madox Ford in *Return to Yesterday*. 'Even if they had been addressing each other from the tribunal of the Academie Française their phrases could not have been more elaborate or delivered more *ore rotundo*. James always addressed Conrad as 'mon cher confrère,' Conrad almost bleated with the peculiar tone that the Marseillais get into their compliments.' James lived just long enough to praise *Chance*, and of all Conrad's works it is, indeed, the one most likely to have attracted him. For in this story, by way of Marlow, Powell and others who report aspects of events, Conrad 'wraps things up.' He uses *oratio obliqua* of every variation. Sub-plot piles on sub-plot until the reader, enthralled if he is technically minded or a puzzle-solver, exasperated if he is not, wonders whether such skill in involution does not at times begin to parody itself. Marlow, usually so self-consistent and convincing, becomes irritable, arch, almost a bore long before the story is over. The query must arise again and again before the end of the book— was all this fuss necessary? Even James wondered why Conrad had piled his difficulties one upon another, and it has been left to Mr. Edward Crankshaw, of a much younger generation, to show by analysis just how clever it all is.

It had proved a difficult book to write. Like *The Rescue* it had been laid aside, not indeed for twenty years, but long enough, and it cannot be said that it shows no signs of struggle. Henry James would have enjoyed them; for he loved scaffolding, one is tempted to think, irrespective of the building to which it is attached. He was a craftsman in love not only with his materials but with his set of tools. Conrad had caught the infection.

With an irony which Conrad savoured, *Chance* (of all his novels published till then perhaps the least likely to be popular), brought him the fame he had missed so long, and fortune enough to last him the rest of his life. It came about through American determination.

Mr. Doubleday, his American publisher, was heartily sick of hearing Conrad praised by all the literary pundits, and gaining wholly disproportionate rewards. He put the whole of his resources of 'promotion'—and they were considerable—behind *Chance*. It had begun serialization in America in 1912, even before it was finished; book publication, planned for 1913, was held up until 1914, so that title-pages and 'condition' have provided a splendid field of dispute for bibliographers. In fact, people were fairly hounded into buying it. As William McFee said in a shrewd address in America in 1938, 'Conrad's fame was artificially stimulated, and he became temporarily celebrated among sections of the public who actually had read very few of his books. . . . This celebrity was followed by an intensive campaign to sell his books to less and less literate publics, as adventure stories of the romantic seas. When these people discovered what kind of stories they had been let in for they laid them aside as "incomprehensible." ' Meanwhile, *Chance* 'went across' in America in a striking way. It was 'required reading' in every self-respecting household. Henceforward, each new book of Conrad's would be an 'event.' He became the fashion among good writers. Mr. Doubleday had, in fact, sold his author as well as this one book.

English circulation gained stimulus from the commotion. When *Chance* appeared, such popular papers as the *Daily Mail* genuflected in its direction; and although a number of discriminating people who had long valued Conrad must have wondered why those who were indifferent before had had their eyes opened by such an unrepresentative commodity, the trick was done. Conrad was no longer a deserving but little-read writer, he was a 'living classic.' The effect was seen even in the tone of his own letters. They became increasingly self-conscious, aware of stature, even at time portentous. To old friends he was the same, but he sometimes spoke like an uncle to strangers, and above all to Americans.

The theme of *Chance* has not much to do with the title. It is that of moral isolation. In Flora de Barral the book has, for once, a heroine who may be said to be at the centre rather than the circumference. She is the daughter of 'the great de Barral,' a financier who has made his fortune by advertising, but behind whom there is not, in truth, much more than warped vanity. De Barral goes smash, and then to prison. The effect upon Flora is catastrophic. She has no mother, and the brutal moral assault of a governess gives her a feeling of being utterly unwanted. Hitherto, she has been petted and sheltered. The cold wind of the world blows in with shattering suddenness, with no reason valid to a child. Nor is her situation made better by a deplorable set of relations; nor yet, in the long run, by the bland household of Fyne in which at one time she seeks refuge. Fyne, that irreproachable Civil Servant, escapes even from the traffic of the London street with a skip of 'purely instinctive precision.' Flora had indeed 'had an ugly pilgrimage.'

She is rescued, and in a sense betrayed, by an officer of the merchant marine, Captain Anthony, 'son of the poet, you know.' If the portrayal of Flora at times stretches credulity, that of Anthony does so continually. He is idealistic, generous, one of those innocent large-hearted men of whom Conrad once said 'the sea, perhaps because of its saltness, roughens the outside but keeps

M

sweet the kernel of its servant's soul.' Anthony 'had set up a standard for himself with that need for embodying in his conduct the dreams, the passion, the impulses the poet puts into the arrangement of verses, which are dearer to him than his own self, and may make his own self appear sublime in the eyes of other people, and even in his own eyes.'

Conrad's portrait is nearly a caricature. 'There are several kinds of heroism,' he says, 'and one of them at least is idiotic. It is the one which wears the aspect of sublime delicacy.' Anthony is so simple that, 'having himself always said exactly what he meant, he imagined that people (unless they were liars) . . . never said more than they meant.'

Anthony enters her life with a sort of predatory tenderness. He does not make her his, for he had 'hit upon that renunciation at which one does not know whether to grin or shudder.' She, for her part, 'beat him at his own honourable game.' 'Bewildered in quivering helplessness by gratuitous cruelty,' she takes the situation as one more result of her unfortunate characteristic of antagonizing people. She sails with Anthony and her father, now released from gaol, in the ample, burnished quarters of the ship *Ferndale*, a wife in name only, but scrupulous in her respect for Anthony's self-imposed conditions.

De Barral loathes the arrangement. He sees in the *Ferndale* merely an extension of his prison. He is jealous for his daughter's love, though he has never taken the slightest trouble to win it. The climax of the story comes when, through a skylight, he is seen by one of the ship's officers (who also loves Flora) to be putting poison in the captain's drink. De Barral commits suicide, after which Flora and Anthony, who have needed each other so long and known each other so little, come together for a well-deserved spell of happiness.

It would not have been in Conrad's nature to conclude conventionally, but he made a considerable effort towards it. Although Anthony is later drowned at sea, it is made quite evident that Flora will never again lack consolation. Her patient lover, Powell, the watcher at the skylight, will have his reward at last.

There are many good scenes in *Chance*, but although it is the delight of the analyst by reason of its complexity, it seems to lack central energy, and to leave at the end the impression of being a display of virtuosity not justified by the theme. It has possibly been responsible, through its wide success, for putting more people off Conrad than any other single work. Considering what riches he has to offer, it was unfortunate that the greater reading public did not come to him through a simpler and more typical story. It is good to know, from Mr. Curle, that Conrad himself 'did not care for *Chance* particularly.'

THE ARROW OF GOLD (1919)

Miss M. C. Bradbrook, in a persuasive study, groups Conrad's work into three periods, the first being 'The Wonders of the Deep' (from *Almayer* to *Typhoon*); the second 'The Hollow Men' (from *Nostromo* to *Victory*); and the third 'Emotion recollected in Tranquillity' (from *The Shadow Line* to the end). Of *The Arrow of Gold*, which was announced with brazen trumpets when it first appeared, one can only say that it represents the emotion without the tranquillity. It was wholly dictated, and bears obvious marks of strain. It is Conrad's least happy novel.

By way of compensation, it tells us something about him, in that it harks back to his youth at Marseilles, and makes a bid to recapture the glamour of Rita, his mysterious Carlist flame, about whom he was always apt to be adjectival. But Rita never achieves life, and the total impression is chiefly that of frustration. Of all his stories, it is the hardest to re-read, and it has found few champions. In his heart of hearts, Conrad was probably not among them. The immediate praise with which the book was greeted must have sounded hollow in his ears, for in truth he was either too far from the atmosphere he tried to call back, or not quite far enough.

THE RESCUE (1920)

The Rescue is Conrad's final impression of Malaya. It was originally intended as the third book in the trilogy in which Lingard appeared. These being written in the reverse of chronological order, it would have been the first in point of time. It belongs, in fact, to the days of Lingard's high summer, and when he is himself on the stage, the scenes lack nothing in vitality. It was begun in 1898, and resumed in 1918, but the marriage between the early and the later material is not an easy one. Nevertheless, it is a good story, and the background was never better.

Its theme is the contrast between sophistication and adventure. Lingard, who with his 'tight ship' is carving out a name for himself in the eastern seas, and who is, in fact, something of a Malayan kingmaker, hears that a yacht is stranded in the shallows off a coast which only he knows well. It contains a party of rich and self-important people, who are oblivious of the real and immediate danger in which they stand. Lingard can rescue them, though only at the cost of his own plans.

He returns, to where the ship lies helpless, in a mood of profound anger. His temper is not made easier by the intolerable attitude of Travers, the owner of the yacht. This man has all the fret and fume of a worldling in circumstances which he can neither control nor understand. On his luxurious little trip he has encountered something real, if local; a matter of life and death, of dynastic war.

For Tom Lingard, there are minor consolations in the stranded party. These are the personalities of an intelligent Spaniard, d'Alcacer, and above all that of Mrs. Travers, who is one of Conrad's 'marvellous women.' It is, in fact, the contrast between Lingard and Mrs. Travers which makes the chief interest of the book. Lingard rightly sees in her something greater than a fashionable woman. As for Lingard, 'he was not mediocre,' thinks Mrs. Travers. 'Whatever he might have been he was not mediocre.' Lingard, for his part, finds Mrs. Travers not merely the most courageous member of the ship's company, but a woman of gaiety and fascination: 'Untouchable, possibly, but remote—no.'

As d'Alcacer says, describing her: 'There are not many of them. And yet they are all. They decorate our lives for us. They are the gracious figures on the drab wall which lies on this side of our common grave. They lead a sort of ritual dance that most of us have agreed to take seriously. . . . Woe to him or her who breaks it. Directly they leave the pageant they get lost . . . lost in a maze. . . . Do you know, Captain Lingard, how people lost in a maze end? . . . They end by hating their very selves, and they die in disillusion and despair.' One thinks instantly, on reading this passage, of the fate of Decoud in *Nostromo*.

After hazards and excitements, the yacht is at last got off the sandbank, and sails away. Lingard is left with a vivid memory, but his Malay friends have been betrayed, and he must seek his adventures elsewhere. As showing an impact between two worlds which can seldom truly mingle, *The Rescue* is a striking book, if in a rather academic manner. Moreover, Conrad was himself at home in both, which cannot always be said either of a romantic, or of a novelist of manners.

*   *   *

No writer, not Shakespeare himself, is always at his best. If Conrad's lesser novels do not approach *Nostromo*, in each one will be found compensatory passages of beauty and wisdom. Moreover, it is often so that a less taxing book than the greatest has a surer immediate appeal. Those who may hesitate at the sight of the icy peak of Higuerota or the squalor of East-end London may yet be charmed, and return again and again, to such stories as *Almayer's Folly* and *The Rescue*. As with Conrad, so with Hardy and other novelists of calibre. How many, awed by the creaking if at times sublime tragedy of *Tess*, have found consolation in the lesser but assured pleasures of *The Trumpet Major*? Conrad had an amiable weakness for some of his minor works, and it has found echoes.

'A man should stand up to his bad luck, to his mistakes, to his conscience and all that sort of thing,' says Captain Giles in *The Shadow Line*, 'why—what else would you have to fight against?' It is by his best that one judges Conrad; he would have expected no less, but the best exacts almost as much as it gives, and with his unswerving devotion to truth, he would never have hoped to rise to it with the regularity of an automaton.

LIFE AND LETTERS

As with most serious artists, Conrad was weaving his autobiography, like a seamless coat, throughout his years as an author. Had he set about it formally, it could scarcely have taken strict chronological shape, since that was not his way of doing things. Although he saw life steadily enough, ordered sequence of event mattered nothing to him, and he knew well that the most vital part of any action is often not the thing itself, but its memory and its delayed effects.

Nevertheless, Conrad had always been aware that the mere facts of his life had been unusual enough to deserve record: hence, first, *The Mirror of the Sea* (1906), then *A Personal Record*, which originally appeared under the title of *Some Reminiscences* (1912); finally, *Notes on Life and Letters* (1921), which were nothing more than a series of collected papers, but had the advantage over *Last Essays* (1926) of being chosen and prefaced by himself.

A Personal Record, an important source-book, has been quoted already and will be referred to later; meanwhile there are certain passages in *Notes on Life and Letters* which are of more than casual interest, since, in his own words, the book shows 'Conrad literary, Conrad political, Conrad reminiscent, Conrad controversial . . . as near as I shall ever come to *deshabillé* in public.'

'Conrad literary' writes of Henry James, Alphonse Daudet, Guy de Maupassant, Anatole France, Turgenev, Stephen Crane, Marryat, Fenimore Cooper and a few less permanent authors. His essays are mostly tributes, and that on James is notable for the phrase 'his mind is steeped in the waters flowing from the fountain of intellectual youth.'

As for Marryat, an early and enduring influence, if only as the creator of 'a priceless legend,' that of Nelson's breed, no one has ever made a shrewder comment about him than that 'he loved his country first, the Service next, the sea perhaps not at all. But the sea loved him without reserve. It gave him his professional distinction and his author's fame—a fame such as not often falls to the lot of a true artist.'

Conrad's remarks on Turgenev are contained in a letter to Edward Garnett, with whom he rarely differed in literary judgments, but whose pleasure in the Russian novelists he could not always share. Turgenev was an exception. 'Every gift has been heaped on his cradle,' he says, 'absolute sanity and the deepest sensibility, the clearest vision and the quickest responsiveness, penetrating insight and unfailing generosity of judgment, an exquisite perception of the visible world, the clearest mind, the warmest heart, the largest sympathy—all that in perfect measure.' It is an interesting passage, as showing that Conrad never allowed a general prejudice to stand in the way of a particular admiration.

'Conrad political' contributes a long and once much studied paper, 'Autocracy and War,' which is an assessment of the Russo-Japanese war of 1905 from the point of view of the defeated country. Conrad then thought Russia, as an expanding power, to be finished, temporarily at least, while he was aware, as never before, of 'the German Eagle with a Prussian head' which 'looks all round the horizon not so much for something to do that would count for good in the records of the earth, as simply for something good to eat.' Russia, he says, 'from the first ghastly dawn of her existence as a State had to breathe the atmosphere of despotism; she found nothing but the arbitrary will of an obscure autocrat at the beginning and end of her organization. Hence arises her impenetrability to whatever is true in Western thought. Western thought, when it crosses her frontiers, falls under the spell of her autocracy, and becomes a noxious parody of itself.' He ends 'Le Prussianisme— voilà l'ennemi!' In the light of the next decades the analysis was acute; while even Conrad could scarcely have been expected to foresee the consequences first of revolution in Russia, brought about by both external and internal pressure, and at last victory due in part to that Western alliance to which she remained so indifferent.

Conrad's Polish papers—both 'political' and 'reminiscent'—consist of four essays, the first on 'The Crime of Partition,' the second a 'Note on the Polish Problem' and the others souvenirs of his visit home in 1914, when the world war burst upon him. In 'The Crime of Partition' he quotes the preamble of a Polish Treaty of Union of 1413. 'It begins,' he says, 'with the words, "This Union, being the outcome not of hatred, but of love"—words that Poles have not heard addressed to them politically by any nation for the last one hundred and fifty years.' Distrusting the declarations of belligerents at the outbreak of war, each side promising Poland what they had, severally, always denied her, he regarded the reconstitution of the country with strictly tempered optimism. As he says in 'Poland Revisited,' 'the most innocent of passions will take the edge off one's judgment,' and he had learnt in years of bitter suffering never to hope too much.

Nothing he actually witnessed in Poland had, in fact,

given him reason to look to the future with any confidence. 'There we remained,' he recalls of his experience when his country appeared trapped by war, and his
family with it, 'unable to obtain permission to travel by
train or road. It was a wonderful, a poignant two
months . . . a whole people seeing the culmination of
its misfortunes in a final catastrophe, unable to trust
anyone, to appeal to anyone, to look for help to any
quarter; deprived of all hope and even of its last illusions,
and unable, in the trouble of minds and the unrest of
consciences, to take refuge in stoical acceptance. I have
seen all this. And I am glad I have not so many years
left me to remember that appalling feeling of inexorable
fate, tangible, palpable, come after so many cruel years,
a figure of dread, murmuring with iron lips the final
words: "Ruin—and Extinction." '

Conrad was never more gloomy, and naturally so.
He was personally anxious, suffering for his family, and
above all he was not of the generation upon which would
fall the task of rebuilding Poland. That would be left to
younger men. As for himself, it was perhaps artistic-
cally fitting that he should have returned to Poland at
one of the last dark moments before her reawakening.

'Conrad reminiscent' was far less tragic about his
adopted country, least of all about her seamen. At the
end of the first world war he summed up, in a very
individual way, the achievement under arms of the
merchant navy. 'The seamen of Great Britain have done
well,' he said. 'In the Navy, where human values are
thoroughly understood, the highest signal of commen-
dation complimenting a ship (that is, a ship's company)
on some achievement, consists exactly of those two
simple words "Well done" followed by the name of the
ship. Not marvellously done, astonishingly done,

wonderfully done—no, only just "well done, so-and-so." ' ' A sailor,' he says in *Chance*, 'is not an adventurer, he is a "sea-farer." ' Conrad was as confident of the future of Great Britain in her ocean trafficking as he was about anything in this transitory life: once again, his view has stood the test of time.

'Gone,' he says in 'The End of the Tether,' 'gone the white-winged flock of clippers that lived in the boisterous uncertain life of the winds, skimming big fortunes out of the foam of the seas': but, in a surprising passage in a 'Conrad controversial' essay (concerning the loss of the *Titanic*) he says of the future, 'we shall have comparatively small crews of disciplined, intelligent workers, able to steer the ship, handle anchors, man boats, and at the same time competent to take their place in the bench as fitters and repairers: the resourceful and skilled seamen-mechanics of the future, the legitimate successors of these seaman-sailors of the past, who had their own kind of skill, hardihood and tradition, and whose last days it has been my lot to share.'

Conrad the realist was not always Conrad the tragedian, for where the essentials of his two professions, letters and the sea, were concerned, he remained supple in mind. Never did the blight of too rigid conservation wither his sympathy. *Laudator temporis acti*—he was sparing of that melancholy tag.

*　　　*　　　*

There is not a great deal in *Last Essays*, a posthumous collection which we owe to Mr. Curle, that Conrad himself would have taken great pains to preserve. A paper on 'Geography and Explorers' is notable for the account of how he took the *Otago* through the Torres Strait, and for a passage about the sea and its travellers which came clearly from the heart. 'The sea,' he said, 'has been for me a hallowed ground, thanks to those books of travel and discovery which have peopled it with unforgettable shades of the masters in the calling which, in a humble way, was to be mine too; men great in their endeavour and in hard-won successes of militant geography; men who went forth each according to his lights and with varied motives, laudable, or sinful, but each bearing in his heart a spark of the sacred fire.'

It is the testament of a romantic adventurer, such as Conrad once had been, a man whose writing is soaked in the sea tradition. Yet Conrad tried hard and long to untie the label of sea-writer which had become so firmly (and, surely, so reasonably) attached to him. In his 'Preface to "Shorter Tales,"' included in the same collection, he wrote: 'As a matter of fact I have written of the sea very little, if the pages were counted. It has been the scene, but very seldom the aim, of my endeavour. It is too late after all these years to keep back the truth; so I will confess here that when I launched my first paper boats in the days of my literary childhood, I aimed at an element as restless, as dangerous, as changeable as the sea, and even more vast—the unappeasable ocean of human life.'

CONCLUSION

'IF you read *A Personal Record* and *Notes on Life and Letters*,' says Sir Desmond MacCarthy in a brief portrait of Conrad, 'you will come nearer to understanding him and the relation in which his way of thinking stood to his work, than by reading his critics.' Although those words were written many years ago, and although shrewd, wise and sympathetic writers have since turned their attention to Conrad, they remain true, for he was as intensely and objectively aware of himself as he was of any of the characters he portrayed with such care. It was as impossible to pull the wool over his eyes, where his own personality was concerned, as it would have been to have deceived him as to the merit of a book or a person. He had learnt about men by reflection, by working with them, and by commanding them. The process was as complete as it could well be.

'He had the kind of manners,' continues Sir Desmond, 'which improve those of a visitor beyond recognition.' And his manners were not superficial, they were the essence of his attitude towards humanity. He gave people value. How rare this quality is, experience teaches all percipient people.

Valuing man, he believed, fundamentally, in mankind. Even Dr. Monyham in *Nostromo*, broken as he had been by torture into betrayal of others, at the end by some miracle retains his integrity. 'It is most unreasonable,' he says to his idol, Mrs. Gould, 'to demand that a man should think of other people so much better than

he is able to think of himself.' Unreasonable, and yet it
happens, since, as Conrad once said in a letter to a friend,
'no circumstance of man's contriving can be stronger
than a personality upheld by faith and conscience.'

*   *   *

A Personal Record is the most episodic of books. It was
first written in answer to a demand, by Ford Madox
Ford, for some reminiscences for *The English Review*.
And since he had already put down so much direct
experience in *The Mirror of the Sea*, what chiefly remained
to be said at that time concerned his early life with his
father, his ambition to go to sea, and just how he set
about achieving it. There were also some reflections on
the life of an author, particularly when engaged on such
a great task as *Nostromo*.

The many asides include long dissertations on his
family's part in the great Continental land campaigns of
the time of Napoleon, and much about the revolutionary
spirit, which for some years had focused his attention.
It is, he said of revolution, 'mighty convenient in this,
that it frees one from all scruples as regards ideas. Its
hard, absolute optimism is repulsive to my mind by the
menace of fanaticism and intolerance it contains.'

Of the many sayings in *A Personal Record*, none are
more deservedly quoted than the sentence about his art:
'He who wants to persuade should put his trust not in
the right argument but in the right word.' And the
other about himself: 'Those who read me,' he says,
'know my conviction that the world, the temporal
world, rests on a few very simple ideas; so simple that
they must be as old as the hills. It rests notably, among
others, on the idea of Fidelity.'

Fidelity is a constituent part of personal honour.

'I contend,' says the French lieutenant in *Lord Jim*, 'that one may get on knowing very well that one's courage does not come of itself. . . . But the honour—the honour, monsieur! . . . that is real, that is! And what life may be worth when . . . the honour is gone . . . I can offer no opinion—because—monsieur—I know nothing of it.'

*   *   *

Conrad is often spoken of as a romantic, but never, rightly, as a romancer. Romance and realism fuse in him as 'an inborn faculty. This,' he says in his Note to *Within the Tides*, 'in itself may be a curse, but when disciplined by a sense of personal responsibility and a recognition of the hard facts of existence, becomes but a point of view from which the very shadows of life appear endowed with an internal glow. And such romanticism is not a sin. It is none the worse for a knowledge of truth. It only tries to make the best of it, hard as it may be; and in this hardness discovers a certain aspect of beauty.' Where he differs from the romancer is that, in his own words, 'I insist not on the events but on their effect upon the persons in the tale.' Evil is true (all too true): good is true; but what matters to Conrad as to any good novelist is their impact upon individual men and women. 'Everybody must walk in the light of his own heart's gospel,' he said early in his writing career, in one of those patient letters he some- times wrote to less gifted people. 'No man's light is good to any of his fellows. That's my view of life—a view that rejects all formulas, dogmas and principles of other people's making.'

'One thing I am certain of is that I have approached the object of my task, things human, in a spirit of piety. The earth is a temple where there is going on a mystery play, childish and poignant, ridiculous and awful enough in all conscience. . . . I've tried to write with dignity, not out of regard for myself, but for the sake of the spectacle, the play with an obscure beginning and an unfathomable *dénouement*.'

'I have been called a writer of the sea, of the tropics, a descriptive writer, a romantic writer—and also an idealist,' he says again, 'but as a matter of fact all my concern has been with the "ideal" value of things, events and people. That and nothing else.'

Above all, he sought clarity. That point he had put directly to Jacques, on that momentous day at sea when he had first revealed a 'work in progress.' It was an admirable Latin trait. 'I want to be read by many eyes and by all kinds of them,' he said to his American publisher. 'I pride myself that there is no sentence of my writing, either thought or image, that is not accessible, I won't say to the meanest intelligence (meanness is a matter of temperament rather) but to the simplest intelligence that is aware of all the world in which we live.'

As for his core, a passage from a letter dating from 1922 is perhaps the most valuable summing up of the many we have. 'Racially,' he said, 'I belong to a group which has historically a political past, with a Western Roman culture derived at first from Italy and then from France, and a rather Southern temperament; an outpost of Westernism with a Roman tradition, situated between Slavo-Tartar Byzantine barbarism on one side and the German tribes on the other; resisting both influences desperately and still remaining true to itself to this very day. I went out into the world, to France and England, and in neither country did I feel myself a stranger for a moment; neither as regards ideas, sentiments, nor institutions.'

He always resented being labelled Slav, and regretted that he had started to build up his reputation just at the time the greater Russian novelists were being 'discovered.' 'As a matter of fact,' he continued, later in the same passage, 'I never knew Russian. The few novels I have read I have read in translation. Their mentality and their emotionalism have been always repugnant to me, hereditarily and individually. Apart from Polish my youth has been fed on French and English literature. While I was a boy . . . we were steeped in classicism to the lips. I am a child, not of a savage but of a chivalrous tradition, and if my mind took a tinge it was from French romanticism perhaps. It was fed on ideas, not of revolt but of liberalism of a perfectly disinterested kind, and on severe moral lessons of national misfortune. . . . In whatever I have achieved afterwards I have simply followed my instinct: the voice from inside.'

Although the voice took long to reach the many to whom Conrad wished to appeal, when it at last did so it was in accents as impressive as they were unfamiliar. They echo yet, and may do so as long as the English novel continues to be read: for the comparative indifference to his work which followed soon after his death is now well past, and rediscovery proceeds apace. He was like no one else. 'Comparisons,' says Dogberry in *Much Ado*, 'are odorous.' They are also unnecessary, since he left no 'school' and derived from none.

He even disclaimed Flaubert. 'I don't think I learned anything from him,' he wrote to Hugh Walpole in 1918. 'What he did for me was to open my eyes and arouse my admiration. One can learn something from Balzac, but what can one learn from Flaubert? He compels admira-

N

tion—about the greatest service one artist can render another.'

Most important of all, he was a good European, of a type which, rare in Western literature, will, it is to be hoped, be found increasingly in the future; a man whose work transcends purely national barriers. He knew and loved England, France and Poland with an affection as deep as it was faithful: above all, their people. 'The greatest figure of the times through which we have lived,' he wrote to Sir Sidney Colvin during the first war, is 'the People itself, *la Nation*. For the last hundred and fifty years the French people has always been greater (and better) than its leaders, masters and teachers. And the same can be said of the English.' Time has endorsed still further another of his verdicts.

* * *

Of Conrad as a personality there are intimate full-scale portraits. There is that by his wife; by his collaborator in earlier years, Ford Madox Ford; and by a younger friend, Mr. Richard Curle. His wife wrote most intimately; Ford recorded the years of struggle and anxiety; Mr. Curle his success, when that constant worry for his family had begun to lift, only to be replaced with concern at the fragility of his wife's health. The accounts agree in one material matter, that Conrad was the most lovable man the writers had ever known. At times irascible, given to moods and silences, extravagant, capable of prejudice, his essential nature was one of sustained affection, of rare warmth, generosity and wisdom. He did not admit mean or narrow thought; and his conversation and way of telling a story were consummate.

There can be no doubt that, as a writer, Conrad owed some debt to Ford. Over a period of years they *thought*

together, and had much in common. Ford cared as
greatly as Conrad for the sheer art of writing, and it was
to suggestions made by him that were due the theme of
The Secret Agent, and important passages in *Nostromo*.
Moreover, *Romance*, their joint work, is one of distinction, the result of several years of planning. Ford
had the great advantage of being at home in the French
language, and, recalling that this was equally true of
Conrad, it made an important point in common.

Mr. Curle's account, although it is not one of the
relationship between master and pupil, since Mr. Curle
is not a professional novelist, naturally shows the effect
of a considerable difference in years. It is specially
pleasing for the light it throws on Conrad's belief in
younger people. It is a touching record of a man blessed
in success, one who retained his vivid interest in men
and affairs to the very last day of his life.

> . . . Speak of no man's happiness
> Till without sorrow he hath passed the goal of life.

So says Oedipus the King. Sorrow is the general lot
which none are spared: but to keep fresh the love of life
and people until the end is one great source of spiritual
refreshment.

There are many valedictory passages which could be
quoted, with perfect fitness, from Conrad's own vivid
prose. Many have already served their turn, and it would
be superfluous to repeat them. But he once wrote a
preface to a handbook of cookery compiled by his wife,
wherein these words occur: 'The decency of our life is
for a great part a matter of good taste, of the correct
appreciation of what is fine in simplicity.' The phrase
'good taste' has, alas, become debased, but as Conrad

N*

used it, it is as full of meaning which can be applied to himself as is the word 'simplicity.' Both express him.

He was a man of fine perceptions, fine taste, and a writer of a flavour which is unlikely to recur. His complexities are shown in his superb craft, but it is his simplicities which make him enduring.

THE *WIADOMOSCI* INQUIRY

FIVE and twenty years after Conrad's death, in 1949, the Polish paper *Wiadomosci* (published in London) sought the views of about fifty men and women of letters as to his place in literature.

Of those who were familiar with Conrad's work, twelve would not venture to prophesy; some indeed doubted if there was any such thing as permanence in letters; but thirty declared for classical rank, and there were only two dissentients. Among works chosen as likely to last longest, twelve emphasized the claim either of *Under Western Eyes* or *The Secret Agent*, a reversal of all but the most acute earlier judgment. Most, who knew Conrad's work well, remarked on his exoticism, and only rarely was there unawareness of his Polish origin and his French associations.

Several writers, including Mr. Henry Baerlein and Mr. Robert Graves, remarked that he wrote English 'too well.' Miss Phyllis Bottome, in a shrewd criticism, emphasized (as did many others) his excellence in 'sea affairs.' Conrad's novels, she said, 'give the effect of a perfectly designed Byzantine mosaic—sparkling, distinct, and emotionally unresponsive to the awed spectator. I think,' she added, 'it was when Conrad was most a Pole that he was at his best as an English author.'

Mr. Louis Golding placed Conrad with Scott and above Stevenson (which would have pleased him). Professor J. B. S. Haldane said: 'He wrote of men and women in situations which will interest readers a hundred years hence, for example sailors, revolutionaries, colonial exploiters.' Mr. George Orwell remarked on his 'political understanding'; Mr.

G. D. H. Cole that he was 'the interpreter of one half of Europe to the other.'

The inquiry was unique of its kind. It inspired a great deal of thoughtful comment, and its greatest value was, perhaps, as a sign of keen revival in critical attention. Such a symposium, originating from Poles in exile after a European cataclysm, would have appealed to that melancholy irony which was so much a part of Conrad.

SELECT BIBLIOGRAPHY

(Place of publication London, unless stated otherwise.)

Bibliographies:

A CONRAD LIBRARY, collected by T. J. Wise (1928)

A CONRAD MEMORIAL LIBRARY, The Collection of G. K. Keating, New York (1929); with 'A Check List of Editions.' (1938) by J. T. Babb (New Haven: Yale).

Collected Editions:

THE WORKS OF JOSEPH CONRAD, 20 vols. Heinemann (1921–7).

THE UNIFORM EDITION OF THE WORKS OF JOSEPH CONRAD, 22 vols. Dent (1923–8).
Contains Conrad's Prefaces, and is complete except for the plays and *The Nature of a Crime* (1924).

THE MEDALLION EDITION, 22 vols. Gresham Publishing Co. (1925).
Follows the Uniform edition and includes illustrations.

THE COLLECTED EDITION OF THE WORKS OF JOSEPH CONRAD, Dent (1946, continuing).
Reprinted from the Uniform edition.

Separate Works:

ALMAYER'S FOLLY—A Story of an Eastern River (1895). *Novel.*

AN OUTCAST OF THE ISLANDS (1896). *Novel.*

THE NIGGER OF THE 'NARCISSUS'—A Tale of the Sea (1897). *Novel.*

TALES OF UNREST (1898). *Short Stories.*
Contains: 'Karain: a Memory,' 'The Idiots,' 'An Outpost of Progress,' 'The Return,' 'The Lagoon.'

LORD JIM—A Tale (1900). *Novel.*

THE INHERITORS—An Extravagant Story (1901). *Novel.*
In collaboration with Ford Madox Hueffer.

YOUTH—A Narrative: and Two Other Stories (1902).
Short Stories.
Contains: 'Youth,' 'Heart of Darkness,' 'The End of the
Tether.'

TYPHOON, and Other Stories (1903). *Short Stories.*
Contains: 'Typhoon,' 'Amy Foster,' Flak,' 'Tomorrow.'

ROMANCE—A Novel (1903). *Novel.*
In collaboration with Ford Madox Hueffer.

NOSTROMO—A Tale of the Seaboard (1904). *Novel.*

THE MIRROR OF THE SEA—Memories and Impressions (1906).
Autobiography.

THE SECRET AGENT—A Simple Tale (1907). *Novel.*

A SET OF SIX (1908). *Short Stories.*
Contains 'Gaspar Ruiz,' 'The Informer,' 'The Brute,'
'An Anarchist,' 'The Duel,' 'Il Conde.'

UNDER WESTERN EYES (1911). *Novel.*

SOME REMINISCENCES (1912). *Autobiography.*
This title appears in the Collected Editions as *A Personal
Record.*

'TWIXT LAND AND SEA—Tales (1912). *Short Stories.*
Contains: 'A Smile of Fortune,' 'The Secret Sharer,'
'Freya of the Seven Isles.'

CHANCE—A Tale in Two Parts (1914). *Novel.*

VICTORY—An Island Tale (1914). *Novel.*

WITHIN THE TIDES—Tales (1915). *Short Stories.*
Contains: 'The Planter of Malata,' 'The Partner,' 'The
Inn of the Two Witches,' 'Because of the Dollars.'

THE SHADOW LINE—A Confession (1917). *Novel.*

THE ARROW OF GOLD—A Story between Two Notes (1919).
Novel.

THE RESCUE—A Romance of the Shallows (1920). *Novel.*

NOTES ON LIFE AND LETTERS (1921). *Essays.*

THE ROVER (1923). *Novel.*

THE SECRET AGENT—A Drama in Four Acts (1923).

THE NATURE OF A CRIME (1924)

A fragment of a story, in collaboration with Ford Madox Hueffer. Includes an 'Appendix': A Note on *Romance* recalling details of the collaboration of 1903.

LAUGHING ANNE and ONE DAY MORE (1924). *Drama.*

One-act plays: the first from the story 'Because of the Dollars'; the second from 'Tomorrow.' Introduction by John Galsworthy.

SUSPENSE—A Napoleonic Novel (1925). *Novel.*

Uncompleted at Conrad's death.

TALES OF HEARSAY (1925). *Short Stories.*

Contains: 'The Warrior's Soul,' 'Prince Roman,' 'The Tale,' 'The Black Mate.' Preface by R. B. Cunninghame Graham.

LAST ESSAYS (1926). Introduction by Richard Curle. *Essays.*

THE NIGGER OF THE 'NARCISSUS', TYPHOON and THE SHADOW LINE, edited by A. J. H. [oppé]. (1945).

Printed in one volume, No. 980, in Everyman's Library.

FOUR TALES: 'The Nigger of the 'Narcissus',' 'Youth', 'The Secret Sharer' and 'Freya of the Seven Isles', with an Introduction by Sir David Bone (1949).

Printed in one volume, No. 518, in The World's Classics.

THE LIFE AND LETTERS OF JOSEPH CONRAD, 2 vols. Edited by G. Jean-Aubry (1927).

The principal source-book for the details of Conrad's life and friendships.

JOSEPH CONRAD'S LETTERS TO HIS WIFE with a Preface by Jessie Conrad (1927).

LETTERS FROM CONRAD, 1895–1924. Edited with an Introduction by Edward Garnett (1928).

CONRAD TO A FRIEND: LETTERS FROM JOSEPH CONRAD TO RICHARD CURLE (1928). Edited with an Introduction and Notes by Richard Curle.

LETTRES FRANÇAISES par Joseph Conrad. Edité par G. Jean-Aubry. Paris (1930).

LETTERS OF JOSEPH CONRAD TO MARGUERITE PORADOWSKA.
Translated from the French and edited by John A. Gee
and Paul J. Sturm. New York (1940).

French : A Series of volumes translated under the editorship of
André Gide and G. Jean-Aubry:

LA FOLIE-ALMAYER. Trans. G. Séligmann-Lui. Paris.
UN PARIA DES ÎLES. Trans. G. Jean-Aubry.
LE NÉGRE DE 'NARCISSUS.' Trans. Robert D'Humèires. Paris.
LORD JIM. Trans. P. Neel. Paris.
FORTUNE. Trans. P. Neel. Paris.
TYPHON. Trans. André Gide. Paris.
NOSTROMO. 2 vols. Trans. P. Neel. Paris.
SOUS LES YEUX D'OCCIDENT. Trans. P. Neel. Paris.
UNE VICTOIRE. Trans. Isabelle Rivière and P. Neel. Paris.
EN MARGE DES MARÉES. Trans. G. Jean-Aubry. Paris.

Also :

HOMMAGE A JOSEPH CONRAD, 1857–1924. Essays by various
writers, Paris (1924).
VIE DE CONRAD par G. Jean-Aubry, Paris (1947).
The preliminary material contains a useful list of trans-
lations of stories made by Conrad's French biographer,
and the text some additional letters.
SAGESSE DE CONRAD. Textes choisis par G. Jean-Aubry,
Paris (1947).

Polish : Translation of Conrad's work into Polish has been
extensive. A Collected Edition was published in Warsaw
between 1923 and 1939 in 28 volumes, the principal
translator being Aniela Zagorska. There have been other
series; and some translation has been resumed since the war.
Polish studies include:

ZE STUDJOW NAD JOSEPHEM CONRADEM (Studies of Joseph
Conrad). Zbigniew Grabowski (1927).
ZYWIOL MORSKI W TWORCZOSCI JOZEFA CONRADA (The Sea
in Conrad's Works). Roman Dybowski (1932).

PIERWIASTKI ANGIELSKIE I PIERWIASTKI POLSKI W UMY-
SLOWOSCI JOSEPHA CONRADA (English and Polish Elements
in Conrad's Character). Roman Dybowski (1933).

JOSEPH CONRAD W POLSCE (Joseph Conrad in Poland).
Piotr Grzegorozyk (1933).

O KONRADZIE KORZENIOWSKIM (Joseph Conrad). Josef
Ujejski (1936).

O CONRADZIE I KIPLINGU (On Conrad and Kipling). Jan
Perlowski (1937).

Translations of Conrad's works have appeared in all the
principal European languages.

Some Critical and Biographical Studies:
 JOSEPH CONRAD, A Study by Richard Curle (1914).
 NOTES ON NOVELISTS, by Henry James (1914).
  Includes an appreciation of Conrad's early work.
 JOSEPH CONRAD, by Hugh Walpole (1916).
 JOSEPH CONRAD, His Romantic Realism, by Ruth M.
  Stauffer (1922).
 AT SEA WITH JOSEPH CONRAD, by J. G. Sutherland (1922).
  Experiences of 1916 in H.M. brigantine *Ready.*
 JOSEPH CONRAD, A Personal Reminiscence by Ford Madox
  Ford (formerly known as Ford Madox Hueffer) (1924).
 THE COMMON READER, by Virginia Woolf (1925).
  Includes a valedictory essay.
 NOTES ON JOSEPH CONRAD, by Arthur Symons (1925).
  Includes a few letters.
 A TALK WITH JOSEPH CONRAD, by R. L. Mégroz (1926).
 JOSEPH CONRAD AS I KNEW HIM, by Jessie Conrad (1926).
  An invaluable appreciation by Conrad's wife.
 CASTLES IN SPAIN, by John Galsworthy (1927).
  Includes reminiscences of Conrad by his oldest English
  literary friend, and a 'Preface to Conrad's Plays.'
 REDEEMED AND OTHER SKETCHES, by R. B. Cunninghame
  Graham (1927).
  Includes 'Inveni Portum,' an account of Conrad's funeral
  at Canterbury.

THE LAST TWELVE YEARS OF JOSEPH CONRAD, by Richard Curle (1928).

The second of two studies of Conrad by a younger friend and critic.

THE POLISH HERITAGE OF JOSEPH CONRAD, by Gustav Morf (1930).

A psychological study.

PORTRAITS, by Desmond MacCarthy (1931).

Includes an essay on Conrad.

RETURN TO YESTERDAY, by Ford Madox Ford (1931).

Supplements Ford Madox Ford's 'Personal Reminiscence' of 1924.

JOSEPH CONRAD'S MIND AND METHOD, by R. L. Mégroz (1931).

Valuable as an Introduction to Conrad: includes a select bibliography. Developed from *A Talk with Joseph Conrad* (1926).

JOSEPH CONRAD AND HIS CIRCLE, by Jessie Conrad (1935).

JOSEPH CONRAD, Some Aspects of the Art of the Novel, by Edward Crankshaw (1936).

CONRAD'S PREFACES TO HIS WORKS, with Introductory Essay by Edward Garnett and a Biographical Note on his father by David Garnett (1937).

This essay should be read together with the personal note contributed by Edward Garnett to *Letters from Conrad*, 1895–1924. Garnett, when reader for Fisher Unwin, recommended publication of Conrad's first novel, *Almayer's Folly*.

JOSEPH CONRAD, ENGLAND'S POLISH GENIUS, by M. C. Bradbrook (1941).

A scholarly analysis of Conrad's work.

CONRAD AND HIS CONTEMPORARIES, by J. H. Retinger (1941).

THE CONRAD READER, Edited by A. J. Hoppé (1946).

Contains a biographical introduction and a large selection from Conrad's stories and other writing. Retitled *The Conrad Companion* (1948).

THE PORTABLE CONRAD, Edited with an Introduction by
  Morton Dauwen Zable, New York (1947).
  Includes an extensive selection from Conrad's Work,
  with full critical apparatus.

THE GREAT TRADITION, by F. R. Leavis (1949).
  Includes a valuable re-estimate of *Victory*, *Chance*, *Nostromo*,
  The Secret Agent, *Under Western Eyes*, and *Heart of Darkness*.
  The debt of the present assessment to the critical stimulus
  of Dr. Leavis is gratefully acknowledged.

THE CAPTAIN'S DEATH BED, by Virginia Woolf (1950).
  A posthumous collection of essays, one of which 'Mr.
  Conrad, a Conversation,' written in 1923, valuably sup-
  plements the author's valedictory essay in *The Common
  Reader*, 1925.

INDEX OF SHORT STORIES

(The title in brackets refers to the volume in which the story appears.)

INDEX OF ESSAYS, ETC.

(The title in brackets refers to the volume in which the essay appears.)

INDEX